The picture dancing on a screen

Wallace Reid's dog Spike, sitting on his master's chair at the studio. His master, of course, will never return—he died of drug addiction while at the height of his popularity in 1923.

The picture dancing on a screen

POETRY OF THE CINEMA

An Anthology Compiled by Anthony Slide

The Vestal Press, Ltd.
P. O. Box 97
Vestal, New York 13851

Also by Anthony Slide

Early American Cinema (1970)
The Griffith Actresses (1973)
The Idols of Silence (1976)
The Big V: A History of the Vitagraph Company (1976; revised 1987)
Early Women Directors (1977; revised 1984)
Aspects of American Film History prior to 1920 (1978)
Films on Film History (1979)
The Kindergarten of the Movies: A History of the Fine Arts Company (1980)
The Vaudevillians (1981)
Great Radio Personalities in Historic Photographs (1982)
A Collector's Guide to Movie Memorabilia (1983)
Fifty Classic British Films: 1932–1982 (1985)
A Collector's Guide to TV Memorabilia (1985)
The American Film Industry: A Historical Dictionary (1986)
Great Pretenders (1986)
Fifty Classic French Films: 1912–1982 (1987)
The Cinema and Ireland (1988)

With Edward Wagenknecht

The Films of D.W. Griffith (1975)
Fifty Great American Silent Films: 1912–1920 (1980)

Editor

Selected Film Criticism: 1896–1911 (1982)
Selected Film Criticism: 1912–1920 (1982)
Selected Film Criticism: 1921–1930 (1982)
Selected Film Criticism: 1931–1940 (1982)
Selected Film Criticism: 1941–1950 (1983)
Selected Film Criticism: Foreign Films 1930–1950 (1984)
Selected Film Criticism: 1951–1960 (1985)
International Film, Radio, and Television Journals (1985)
The Best of Rob Wagner's Script (1985)
Selected Theatre Criticism: 1900–1919 (1985)
Selected Theatre Criticism: 1920–1930 (1985)
Selected Theatre Criticism: 1931–1950 (1986)
Filmfront (1986)
Selected Radio and Television Criticism (1987)
Selected Vaudeville Criticism (1988)

Cover illustration: Louise Fazenda

The title of this book is taken from
Siegfried Sassoon's poem, "Picture-Show"

Library of Congress Cataloging-in-Publication Data

The Picture dancing on a screen.

Bibliography: p.
Includes indexes.
1. Motion pictures—Poetry.   2. American poetry—
20th century.   3. English poetry—20th century.
I. Slide, Anthony.   II. Title: Poetry of the cinema.
PS595.M68P53   1988   811'.5'080357   88-265
ISBN 0-911572-71-6 (soft)

Contents

Illustrations

Acknowledgements

Aside from the obligatory acknowledgements which follow, I would like to thank the staffs of the Margaret Herrick Library of the Academy of Motion Picture Arts and Sciences, the Beverly Hills Public Library, the Studio City Public Library, and the Doheny Memorial Library of the University of Southern California; Q. David Bowers, James Curtis, Amy Gerstler of the Beyond Baroque Foundation, Patricia King Hanson, and Lisa Mosher.

The following poems are reprinted by kind permission of their authors:
The Aristocrat and *Laurel and Hardy* by John Bricuth (John T. Irwin).
Jack the Ripper, Vampire and *In Memory of James Wong Howe* by Charles Higham.
On Viewing Love Crazy by Stuart M. Kaminsky.
Dick Powell and *Ozzie Nelson Dead of Cancer* by Ronald Koertge.
Ode to the Silents by Esther Ralston.
Marilyn Monroe and *The Physical Imperfections of Old Films* by Paul Ramsey.
Nobody Dies Like Humphrey Bogart by Norman Rosten; copyright by Norman Rosten from
  his *Selected Poems*, published by Braziller in 1979.
Sternberg: In Memoriam and *Natani Nez: Print the Legend* by Charles Silver.
Twice as Many Gorillas by Jack Skelley.
In Hollywood by Ian Whitcomb.
The poems, *Oh Mr. Laemmle, Cold Are the Hands of Time* and *O, Father Time, Lay Not Thy Frost,* by Preston Sturges, are published by kind permission and copyright of Sandy Sturges.
To Mr. Mack Sennett, on His Animated Pictures by Morris Bishop. From *The Best of Bishop: Light Verse from The New Yorker and Elsewhere* (Cornell). © 1949, 1977 Alison Kingsbury Bishop. Originally in *The New Yorker.*
To Humphrey Bogart and *Clark Gable,* excerpts from *Cagney on Cagney* by James Cagney. Copyright © 1976 by Doubleday & Company, Inc. Reprinted by permission of the publisher.
The Day I Stopped Dreaming about Barbara Steele from *The Day I Stopped Dreaming about Barbara Steele,* by R.H.W. Dillard. © 1965, 1966 by R.H.W. Dillard. Reprinted by permission of the publisher.
Mae West: The Woman behind Diamond Lil by Wes D. Gehring from *The Journal of Popular Film and Television,* Vol. X, No. 1, Spring 1982, page 72. Reprinted with permission of the Helen Dwight Reid Educational Foundation. Published by Heldref Publications, 4000 Albemarle Street, N.W., Washington, D.C. 20016. Copyright © 1982.
Buster Keaton & The Cops by George Keithley. Reprinted from *Song in a Strange Land* by George Keithley by permission of George Braziller, Inc., New York. Copyright © 1974 by George Keithley.
Epitaph for John Bunny, Motion-Picture Comedian and *Mae Marsh, Motion Picture Actress* by Vachel Lindsay. Reprinted with permission of Macmillan Publishing Company from

Introduction

Provided that one ignores examples of society's regression and negativity, the motion picture is the only pure 20th-century art form. It is, therefore, not surprising that it should have generated so much poetic commentary, from the serious to the comic, from the sublime to the ridiculous, from the simplisitc to the pretentious. The motion picture is both an art form and an entertainment, an industry and a highly personal form of creativity, and so its poetry is equally diverse.

Poetry dealing with the cinema first appeared in the early "fan" magazines, such as *The Motion Picture Story Magazine* (later *Motion Picture Magazine*) and *Photoplay*, and poetry was to remain a staple ingredient of such periodicals—ideally suited for use as "fillers"— from the 'teens through the Thirties. Many regular contributors of articles and interviews to the fan magazines were willing and able to provide poetry when required. Julian Johnson, editor of *Photoplay* from 1915–1919, contributed some items, included here, which are the height of pretention, but which, perhaps, illustrate the lofty ideals which some critics hoped the motion picture might attain.

Few recognized poets contributed to the early "fan" magazines. The first poet to give serious consideration to the cinema was Vachel Lindsay (1879–1931), with his book, *The Art of the Moving Picture*, first published by the Macmillan Company in 1915, and in a revised edition in 1922. Lindsay was a modern-day troubadour, touring the country and reading his own poetry with great eloquence. Very much a poet of his time, Lindsay naturally should have been attracted to a popular entertainment of the period, such as the motion picture, which—thanks in large part to D.W. Griffith's efforts—showed every sign of becoming an art form. Lindsay wrote poems on actor John Bunny and actress Mae Marsh, with whom he was particularly enamoured. In *The Golden Whales of California*, published by the Macmillan Company in 1920, he offers "A Doll's 'Arabian Nights,'" as "A Rhymed Scenario for Mae Marsh when she acts in the new many-colored films" (presumably a reference to either Prizma Color or Technicolor).

The earliest poem in this book is by Will Carleton (1845–1912), who is best remembered—if he is remembered at all—for his ballads of the common life, notably "Over the Hill to the Poor House," which was the basis for at least three films. One of his works also provided what is, I consider, the most beautiful title ever used for a film, "Lines of White on a Sullen Sea," a one-reel American Biograph short directed by D.W. Griffith in 1909.

Aside from the poems of Vachel Lindsay, the earliest of serious poets to be included here is Hilda Doolittle (1886–1961), who was noted for the stark quality of her writing. Her interest in the motion picture probably stems from her friendship with Winifred Ellerman (who wrote under the pen name of "Bryher") and Kenneth Macpherson, who founded the early, intellectual film journal, *Close Up*, in Switzerland in 1927. Hilda Doolittle, often using the initials, "H.D.," was a frequent contributor to the magazine.

Aside from the "fan" magazines, poetry on the cinema appeared in a number of popular periodicals of the twenties and thirties, in particular *Life* and *Rob Wagner's Script*. One

writer whose poetry appeared in both the "fan" and the popular magazines of the day was Margaret E. (Elizabeth) Sangster (1894–1981), who was also a novelist, journalist and scriptwriter.

Critics, such as the English C.A. Lejeune, often utilized poetry in their reviews. Many members of the film industry also tried their hand at poetry, and among those included here are director and screenwriter Preston Sturges, cinematographer Virgil Miller, and actors James Cagney, Gene Lockhart, James Mason, Frank Morgan, Esther Ralston, and Rudolph Valentino. Academics are also poets, as witness contributions from Wes D. Gehring, Stuart M. Kaminsky and Charles Silver. Charles Higham is best known today for his show business biographies on Katharine Hepburn, Bette Davis, Errol Flynn, Orson Welles, and others, but—as three items here illustrate—he is also a poet of note.

Among the major contemporary literary figures who have used the motion picture as a subject, and whose works are represented in this anthology, are John Bricuth, Ronald Koertge, Howard Moss, Sharon Olds, Norman Rosten, and John Updike.

The cinema may not always have been poetic, but it has influenced some three generations of poets, both amateur and professional. No other media can make such a claim. Since D.W. Griffith made *Intolerance* in 1916, the motion picture has advocated tolerance and brotherly love. D.W. Griffith and Lillian Gish have often spoken of film as the universal language, and, as early as April 1919, Julian Johnson was writing blank verse in *Photoplay* on this very subject. How ironic that film, the universal language of peace and tolerance, should be equalled in poetic regard only by writings on war.

Anthony Slide

The picture
dancing
on a screen

The Two Lessons
(At the Moving Picture Show)
by Will Carleton

Near the ne-er-lifted curtain we sat, clasping hands,
And awaited the coming of seas and of lands,
And of forests whose branches bore fruits of surprise,
Springing forth—leafy miracles—plain in our eyes;
And of cities that glistened in wealth-laden camps,
As if fifty Aladdins were there with their lamps;
And the women and children and men! who, tho small
To the objects around them were greatest of all.

There were those that came out of the mansion's rich gates,
Or that nursed in the hovels their loves and their hates;
There were sailors who courted the sea, foul or fair,
There were birdmen who swam thru the treacherous air;
There were people from all of the corners of earth,
With their comedies, tragedies, sorrows, and mirth;
Tho they gave us no sound, tho they spoke not a word,
All they said that was worthy the hearing, was heard.

There was nought but seemed waiting the wizard's command,
All the world to us came, at the touch of a hand.
Still, no treasure that white-stretching canvas would win,
But could fade out as something that never had been.

So I asked, as we came from the dusk-sheltered spot,
"That was surely a picture of life, was it not?
"There is nothing that winsome or lovely may seem,
"But may fade like a vision, and die like a dream."

"Yes, 'tis life acted over," she blithesomely said,
"For it shows there is nothing on earth, that is dead;
"Nought we wish, if our efforts no energy lack,
"But howe'er it may vanish, may some time come back."

(reprinted from The Motion Picture Story Magazine, *May 1911, page 73)*

When the World Was Young
by John William Kellette

The world was very young when Adam fell,
When Sardanapalus felt the touch of death;
Swaddling-garbed, the Persian Cyrus roamed
Before Nineveh crumbled to a breath;
The Thebans felt the Alexander smite—
The Punic war of Hannibal had ceased
The budding hopes of Scipio, until
He hied himself Canusium-ward to feast.
The world was still quite very young, indeed,
When Italy felt Marius' sterling worth;
The world, war-laden, groaned adown the years
Preceding "Peace on Earth" and Jesus' birth.

And all we children of the long ago
Who pored thru pages, as a scholar's task,
Delved for knowledge thru a misty glow,
Because the printed letters were a mask.

The earth was very old when this was changed;
Ohio gave the race a wondrous son—
The peer of all inventors of his day,
And yet it seems his work has but begun.
From out the misty distances of years,
His brain created pictures fraught with life;
Had Edison arrived when Cyrus was a king,
A child could glean the lessons of his strife.
This wizard's art has opened up the graves
And called together tribes that fell to dust,
And brushed aside the mysteries of years
Before the world had felt the money lust.

And children of the future years will sing
Their songs of praise to Edison's name;
"Let there be light," said God, and light there was;
But things were dark till Edison came.

(reprinted from The Motion Picture Story Magazine, *February 1912, page 112)*

To the Motion Picture:
An Appreciation

Marvel of science, mirror of art, product of the ingenuity of man and the inventive power of the mind—we speak to you, the Motion Picture!

Not with the sword, not with the oppression and persecution of cruel might, but with mere human sobs and smiles, you have conquered the world.

You are the struggle and the victory! You are Aspiration and Achievement —Hope and Realization!

You are King in the Land of Mechanical Wonders, supreme in the domain of daring dreams!

Your silence speaks of the genius of man, the strength of his purpose, the courage of his endeavours, and the wealth and worth of his labours. You are the mute voice of progress, the echo of creative potency, the symbol of constructive force.

You are the soul of skill and the spirit of Service, the essence of energy, and the germ of enterprise. You thrill with the common sympathy of the universe, and throb with the throes and thralls of united humanity.

You translate the world's sorrows, and delineate life's joys. You bear the burden of the earth, the load of care and misery and evil, the pathetic definition of futility and fatality; yet you catch the gleam of a sunbeam, the lilt of a song—and we laugh!

YOU TEACH! You distribute knowledge, diffuse the secrets of science and the glories of art; you spread civilization. You bring light where is darkness, and life where is only existence. You banish ignorance; you cheer and comfort.

YOU PREACH! Your pulpit is the hearts of the world, your creed faith and sympathy.

Motion Picture you are great! You are the agent of the age, the messenger of futurity!

You are great—and we are grateful!

(reprinted from The Famous Players Review, *Vol. 1, No. 2, April 1914, back cover)*

Song of the Motion Picture Camera
by Joseph F. Poland

What do you sing of, camera grim—
You that the world in motion know—
Sad lay or glad, peace or battle-hymn?
Then did the camera answer low:

Sweet and clear is the song I sing,
Large is it writ on every screen;
In every heart its echoes ring,
Bringing a peace and a joy serene.
Glance at the crowd now hasting along,
See in their faces pleasure rife;
At the picture show they have heard my song—
They have heard my song of the Joy of Life.

The Joy of Life is the song I sing;
I chant not the tread of marching feet
Of men to war, but instead I bring
The children's footsteps down the street
To the picture show. Poor little tots!
Acting Life's drama 'mid tenement scenes,
They gaze entranced at the beauteous spots
And wondrous sights on the movie screens.

The weary toiler hears my song;
I sing alike to the good and bad,
For I draw no lines in that motley throng—
My only tasks are to make all glad,
To spread clean thoughts and to banish strife,
To strengthen the weary, cheer the sad;
So I sing my song of the joy of life
To man and woman, lass and lad.

Camera, your speech has truth and worth;
No bauble are you, no childish toy.
Yours is a world task—the whole wide earth
Shall join with you in your song of joy.

(reprinted from Motion Picture Magazine, *May 1915, page 104)*

Photoplayer Wochy
by L.N. Collier

'Twas Williams and the Kerrigan
Did Cruze and Clayton in the Shay;
Al Wilson was the Pauline Bush,
The sky was Betty Gray.

"Beware the CourtenayFoote, my son,
The AliceJoyce, the GertMcCoy,
The EarleMetcalf, the Richardson,
Beware them all, my boy."

He took his Briscoe sword in hand,
Long time the Wilbur foe he sought;
Then Ostriched he the Sterling band
And Baggoted in thought.

And as in Pickford thought he stood,
The CourtenayFoote, with eyes aflame,
Blackwelled out of the BillGarwood
And Traversed as it came.

Oh, ArtJohnson and Morrison!
His Briscoe sword went snickersnack;
He left it dead and with its head
He Henry Walthalled back.

And hast thou slain the CourtenayFoote?
It is quite Bayne, my Boardman boy.
"Pearl White! Lill Gish! Honk! toot-toot!"
He Gordoned in his joy.

(reprinted from Motion Picture Supplement, *Vol. I, No. 2, October 1915, page 17)*

Lillian and Dorothy Gish

To Lillian and Dorothy Gish and Their Mother
by Francis William Sullivan

The dawn wind, running with fairy feet
Along the floor of the sea;
The dewy essence of meadowsweet,
A sun-wrought witchery;
And mothering earth, who gave them birth—
These are the pictured three.

Fugitive Spring's imprisoned there,
Never to fade or die;
And Autumn, reaping its harvest fair,
Under an azure sky;
Youth's splendid dream, the dare supreme,
And wisdom's grave reply.

Could one but film that dream of youth
That trembles half-awake,
What virgin pleas and mysteries
The camera would take!
And what, if one could see it run,
A movie it would make!

(reprinted from Motion Picture Supplement, *Vol. I., No. 2, October 1915, page 64)*

John Bunny

Epitaph for John Bunny, Motion-Picture Comedian
*(In which he is remembered in similitude, by reference to Yorick,
the king's jester, who died when Hamlet and Ophelia
were children)*
by Vachel Lindsay

Yorick is dead. Boy Hamlet walks forlorn
Beneath the battlements of Elsinore.
Where are those oddities and capers now
That used to "set the table in a roar"?

And do his bauble-bells beyond the clouds
Ring out, and shake with mirth the planets bright?
No doubt he brings the blessed dead good cheer,
But silence broods on Elsinore tonight.

That little elf, Ophelia, eight years old,
Upon her battered doll's staunch bosom weeps.
("O best of men, that wove glad fairy-tales.")
With tear-burned face, at last the darling sleeps.

Hamlet himself could not give cheer or help,
Though firm and brave, with his boy-face controlled.
For every game they started out to play
Yorick invented, in the days of old.

The times are out of joint! O cursed spite!
The noble jester Yorick comes no more.
And Hamlet hides his tears in boyish pride
By some lone turret-stair of Elsinore.

(written in 1915)

History from the Screen
by Oliver E. Behymer

The future historian who writes of our times,
Our social endeavors, our foibles and crimes,
Will find ready-made the material he needs
To interpret the motives that prompted the deeds.
'Tis simple: thru pictures the past lives again;
What he sees with his eyes, he records with his pen.

The kangaroo walk and the new spineless pose;
All the late innovations in dances and clothes;
The hats and the coiffures milady prefers;
All the feminine charms inexpressibly hers,
Will be there for the writer who seeks to portray
A living account of the life of today.

Time shall not crumble our age at a breath;
We shall live with a spirit that's stronger than death;
And the men of tomorrow shall have handed down
A pageant of deeds and a wealth of renown—
Thru the god who resides in a perfect Machine,
We shall live as we are in the Soul of the Screen.

(reprinted from Motion Picture Magazine, *January 1916, page 92)*

I Am the Motion Picture
by Arthur James

I am the Motion Picture.

I am the child of man's genius, the triumph of man over space and time. I am a mute, but I am eloquent to millions. I traverse prairies, glaciers, jungles, forests, sea and air and bring the visions of my journeys to the eyes of common men.

I am the pleasant hour of prince and child, of master mind and little boy. I instruct, I delight, I thrill, I entertain, I please, I shock, I cheer, I move the world to laughter and tears.

I am the sublime story teller of all the ages. I am the drama's greatest brother.

I have more friends than all the friendly men of Earth. I stir the blood, I quicken the pulses, I encourage the imagination, I stimulate the young, I comfort and I solace the old and sorrowing.

I bring priceless Gifts and make them yours.

I show more of travel than all the books penned by all the writers of the world. I preach sermons to congregations, greater than the combined flocks of the pulpits of all lands, I make happiness, I make kindliness. I am the one great International friend.

I am history, written for generations to come in a tongue that every race and sect and creed can understand. I preserve heroes for posterity. I give centuries more of life to the arts and sciences. I am man's greatest and noblest invention.

I am the Motion Picture.

(distributed by Metro Pictures to theatres throughout the United States in the Spring of 1916)

Contentment
by Erroll Hay Colcock

Without a gray and wintry sky,
Pale moonbeams slanting thru;
Within (enough to satisfy),
A photoplay and *you*!

(*reprinted from* Motion Picture Magazine, *December 1916)*

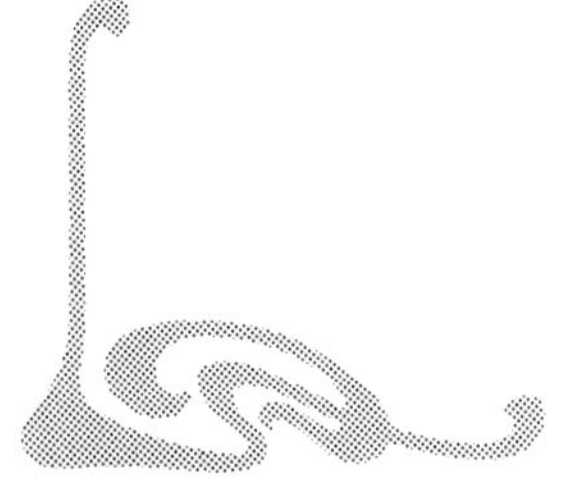

I Am the Motion Picture
by Julian Johnson

I am the Motion Picture.

My feet flounder in the clay, but my head is above the clouds, and my eyes are with the stars.

I am the friend of the humble, the servant of the scholar, the jester of the wise. I am youth to the aged, a gateway to the imprisoned, adventure to the indolent, forgetfulness to the sorrowing, calm to the impatient, rest to the weary.

I am the commonest of common things. I am art for the artless, buffoonery for buffoons, braggadocio for cowards. I revel in backstairs romance. I am the coarse snuggling friend of kitchen mechanics, perfumed and unbathed. My delight is a silly hero of clammy virtue and patent-leather hair. I teach cheap yawps that the fade-out hug solves every problem in the universe. I am a cog-wheeled idol whose temples are redolent of chewing gum and poisonous candy. My services demand music; I have none of my own; I steal everyone's music, and blend it in a horrible mess. I am the matinee idol of slatternly wives, the dime novel of defective boys. I am opium to ambition. I am the drama's illegitimate child. I am literature's idiot brother.

I am the profoundest possibility of modern times. I am one day old—and on my brow the sages have already found the seal of immortality. My eyes are so strong that I see over the rim of the world. I am the only creature who has made Time turn his hour-glass over. I am the imagination of the surgeon and the chart of the doctor. I am the incomparable salesman and the ultimate newspaper. I am magic ink for the shy poet. I am breathing beauty and living virility for the romancer who has known only the pale puppets of words. I am a flash of lightning above the gloomy forest of history. I am the awful mask of war. I am the alchemist of invention. I am the magic carpet and Aladdin's lamp. I am the supreme teacher of the child.

My future is bounded by infinity.

My feet flounder on the clay, but my eyes are with the stars.

I am The Motion Picture.

(reprinted from Photoplay, *Vol. XI, No. 4, March 1917, page 54)*

15

I Am Humanity
by Julian Johnson

I am Humanity.

Sometimes I gaze out at you from your screens and you laugh and weep and applaud Me. Why do you not let Me come oftener to you?

I am the Great Shadow of you—and you—and you—and you. I am the enduring enchantment because I am the only enduring mystery. You have weighed the stars and drained the seas and harnessed the lightning and torn every secret from the breast of the world—but I baffle you, as I shall always baffle you. I am neither good nor bad, lofty nor mean, kind nor spiteful, finite nor eternal—I am at once all of these, yet not any of them.

Every day you flock to your screens to find Me, yet you do not often find Me. And I stand waiting for some One to unlock the doors of light that I may come to you.

Ceaselessly you ask for Me and they give you instead White Puppets and Black Silhouettes, Sugar Girls and Vinegar Vixens, poison slices of a horrible white saccharine they call Life.

I am not only the Father of Progress, but I am the Inspiration of all Art. My life is red and living, not white and dead—My heights are glorious because they are hardly won—when I Love they know it in Heaven; when I Hate they feel it in Hell.

I stand waiting for some One to unlock the door of light.

I am Humanity.

(reprinted from Photoplay, Vol. XII, No. 4, September 1917, page 50*)*

Mae Marsh in *The Birth of a Nation* (1915)

Mae Marsh, Motion Picture Actress
by Vachel Lindsay

The arts are old, old as the stones
From which man carved the sphinx austere.
Deep are the days the old arts bring:
Ten thousand years of yesteryear.

She is madonna in an art
As wild and young as her sweet eyes:
A frail dew flower from this hot lamp
That is today's divine surprise.

Despite raw lights and gloating mobs
She is not seared: a picture still:
Rare silk the fine director's hand
May weave for magic if he will.

When ancient films have crumbled like
Papyrus rolls of Egypt's day,
Let the dusk speak: "Her pride was high,
All but the artist hid away:

"Kin to the myriad artist clan
Since time began, whose work is dear."
The deep new ages come with her,
Tomorrow's years of yesteryear.

(written in 1917)

A Eulogy to "Little Mary"
by Arthur C. Brooks

Mary Pickford,
"Somewhere in Los Angeles,"
Cal.
My dear "Little Mary":
Some years ago, ten
Or twelve, perhaps,
When I was a mewling,
Irrelevant, useless
School-lad, you first
Broke into pictures.
Say, Mary, I fell
Like a Germance "Ace" with
A bullet thru his gas-tank
For you.
I used to haunt the
Scenic Temple
Every Friday night.
Gee, Mary, didn't I love you!
Oh, gosh!
The pictures were rotten
(Mechanically, that is;
Remember how they flic-kik-ered?),
But I didn't mind as long as you
Graced them.
Then you stopped appearing,
I think, for months.
(You once returned to
The "legit" for a time, yes?)
But I kept on going to the movies,
Hoping.
And one night you came back again,
Prettier still.
Gee! I just skipped from cloud to cloud,
Cloud to cloud.
And my eyes shone.
And I breathed like a horse with
Heaves.

Then two matronly ladies,
Probably from Somerville, Mass.,
Complimented you, and one said it was
Too bad that was your last
Picture. . . .
That you had been run down and
Killed by an automobile!
Gee, Mary, somebody turned out the light!
I was broken, cruelly, and stabbed to
The heart.
For centuries and centuries I groped
In Stygian byways, it seemed,
A recluse from inane, incomprehending
People, boobs!

Then you came back again.
And I knew the old hen was a liar!
Well, that's about all, Mary.
I'm glad it didn't happen.
(And I guess you are, too.)
But some time afterwards
A maundering, tactless imbecile
Told me you were married.
O-o-o-o-o, Mary!
Oh, sweet Death!
That's all, Mary.
Just a little appreciation
Of the immeasurable service
You are doing the people.
You are helping to polish
The pewter of their lives.
Well, so long, Mary.
Thanks!

(reprinted from Motion Picture Magazine, *July 1918, page 35)*

I Am the Universal Language
by Julian Johnson

I am the Universal Language.
I call every man in the world Brother, and he calls me Friend.
I have unlocked the riddle of Babel after fifty centuries of misunderstanding.
I am the Voice of Home to Democracy's lonely sentinels on Liberty's frontier.
I am a chorus of Eagle and Lion and Cock, crying "Shame!" to the Bolshevik
Bear.
I am the rising murmur of repentance on lips of the Kingdom of Sin.
I am California, springing a funny story on Constantinople.
I am a Chinese poet of a thousand years ago, singing gently in Chicago.
I am a salesman purveying harvesters, tractors, overalls, oil stoves and hog
products to the Siberians.
I am a vertical and eternal Peace Table, and my Conference has five hundred
million delegates.
I am a tenement doctor, telling mothers of twenty races how to wash their
babies' milk-bottles.
I am the rusty tongue of Rameses, thrilling Broadway with the sunbright story
of my lotus-columned temples on the Nile.
I am the voice of Christ in the country of Confucius.
I am the remembrance of Old Age.
I am the chatter of children with blue eyes or almond eyes.
I am the shy confession of Miss and Ma'amselle and Senorita.
I am a Caspian fisherman, visiting a coffee planter in Santos.
I am the Apostle of Kindness, the Orator of Tolerance, the Minstrel of Love.
I am the greatest Story-Teller of the Ages.
I am the Universal Language.
I am the Motion Picture.

(reprinted from Photoplay, Vol. XV, No. 5, April 1919, page 27*)*

The Rubaiyat of the Screen
by Wanda Hawley*

Wake! for the day with sun is shining bright;
Exterior scenes remain which must be shot by night.
Assemble at the studio by eight o'clock,
Made up and ready, and be sure your costume's right.

Whether at Hollywood or Edendale,
Whether the part you play be fresh or stale,
Be ready when the director's voice you hear;
This is the starting—and you must not fail.

There was a door to which I found no key,
My dressing room tight locked I found—ah, me!
Then props arrived and battered down the door;
With anxious eyes I watched the minutes flee.

But half made up, I hastened to the street
And in the waiting auto took my seat;
Soon we were rumbling down the boulevard,
Bound for some woodland's shadowy retreat.

Arrived at last, the cameras set and all
The players waiting for the master's call,
I, trembling, took my place and acted till
I heard some one who whispered, "Go on, stall!"

Indeed, the idols I had loved so well
Sometimes were shattered; there I shall not tell
All that I learnt; my voice is mute,
And o'er me still the movies cast their spell.

Some fame I've gained upon the shadow screen
That recompenses me for years between,
When long ago I labored and it seemed in vain
Some trace of harvest from the soil to glean.

And when, like others, I one day shall pass
Out of the minds of those I pleased, alas!
I only pray that some one, just for old times' sake,
Shall speak my name—turn down an empty glass!

(reprinted from Motion Picture Magazine, *April 1919, page 70)*

*Wanda Hawley (1895–1963) was on screen from 1917 through 1931; her features include *The Affairs of Anatol* (1922), *The Young Rajah* (1923), *Smouldering Fires* (1925), and *Graustark* (1926).

Wanda Hawley

Picture-Show
by Siegfried Sassoon

And still they come and go; and this is all I know—
That from the gloom I watch an endless picture-show,
Where wild or listless faces flicker on their way,
With glad or grievous hearts I'll never understand
Because time spins so fast, and they've no time to stay
Beyond the moment's gesture of a lifted hand.

And still, between the shadow and the blinding flame,
The brave despair of men flings onward, ever the same
As in those doom-lit years that wait them, and have been—
And life is just the picture dancing on a screen.

(first published 1920)

The Misunderstood Sisterhood
by Delight Evans

By this we Mean
One of
Those Long Ladies
With Lots of Hair
Who Saves the Little Sister
From a Calling-down
By her Irate Husband.
She Always
Takes the Blame.
Greater Glory
Hath no Film Actress
Than that
She Hide her Little Sister
When the Husband Comes—
And while
Little Sister Suffocates
In the Bad Boudoir
Of the Other Man (the Little Dear
Always Rolls herself Up
In the Priceless Persians—you'd think
She'd Smother—too bad she doesn't)
The Misunderstood,
With a Joan of Arc Expression
Steps Out to Face the Music
Sung
In an Uncertain Falsetto
By the
Irate Husband.
The Little Sister
Is Blonde—a
Fluffy Little Thing who is
Rather Well Worth
Sacrificing for,
If you Ask the Audience.
Her Honor
Is More Precious than the Heroine's:
Don't Ask us why, but
She's Chemically Chaste.

So the Heroine
Never Hesitates: she
Gives, and
Gives, and
Gives.
(Sometimes we Wonder
Why it is More Blessed
To Give than to Receive.)
With a Tortured Soul—she Looks it—
She Goes Bravely On, even
Letting the Man who Loves her
Think the Worst.
We Know he Does;
The titles Say So, with
Little Flames of Jealousy
Simply Burning him Up.
The Other Man, whose
Chief Occupation is
Badgering Fluffy Blondes and
Making them
Draw their Capes about them
In Injured Innocence—
(They Always
Go into the Night
In Capes—they've Got to Do it—
It's in their Contracts—)
The Other Man
Breaks his Long Rule
Against Brunettes
And there's a Misty Close-Up
of Him, Narrowing his Eyes.
And we Know
That the Poor Misunderstood
Is in for It.
She'll Do her Old Familiar Act
Of Saving the Family Name.
Ah—but Wait!
The Hero
Has Penetrated the Plot—
(With the Aid of Two
Detective Agencies)
And he Appears to
Blame the Blonde,

Hit the Husband, and
Hug the Heroine—sometimes we wish
It was the Other Way Around.
The Other Man? Oh, he
Goes his Wasteful Way
To Be the Awful Angle
Of another Triangle—you'll meet him
In the Next
Problem Picture you see.
And the Picture Ends—
As it was bound to do—
Sooner or Later—
In a Cradle Close-up, and
A Tearful Title that Says:
"And so
With the Soft Light
of Motherhood
In her Eyes, our
Heroine Looks Forward
To the Dawn
of a Happy New Day."
She has Nothing on Us.

(reprinted from Photoplay, *Vol. XXI, No. 5, April 1922, page 74)*

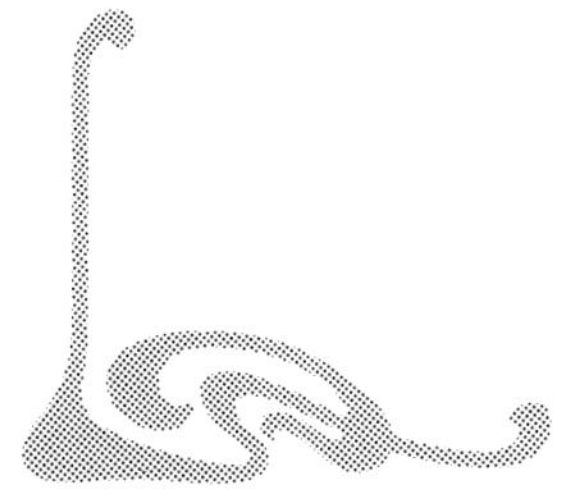

We Make the Movies
(With Apologies to Cock Robin!)

The Producer:
I make the movies!
From my desk I produce 'em,
Like furies unloose 'em,
I make the movies.

The Writer:
I make the movies!
My typewriter rattles
Through death, love and battles—
I make the movies.

The Director:
I make the movies!
My megaphone made me
(Directing has paid me!)
I make the movies.

The Heroine:
I make the movies!
The heroine flighty
In bed, bathroom, nightie!
I make the movies.

The Hero:
I make the movies!
Well tailored and bored,
I'm the hero—my gawd!
I make the movies.

The Cinematographer:
I make the movies!
The stars groan and mutter
At me and my shutter!
I make the movies.

The Ingenue:
I make the movies!
I've my honor and rouge,
Just like all ingenues—
I make the movies.

The Press Agent:
I make the movies!
The press-agent, I—
How my adjectives fly!
I make the movies.

The Art Director:
I make the movies!
I make them artistic
And foolish and mystic.
I make the movies.

The Title Writer:
I make the movies!
Without no fine grammar
My titles—they stammer . . .
I make the movies.

The Prop Maker:
I make the movies!
With hammer and nails
When each soft method fails,
I make the movies.

The Public:
I am the PUBLIC . . .
With endurance and dimes
I buy lemons and limes—
I make the movies.

(reprinted from Photoplay, *Vol. XXIII, No. 2, January 1923, page 62)*

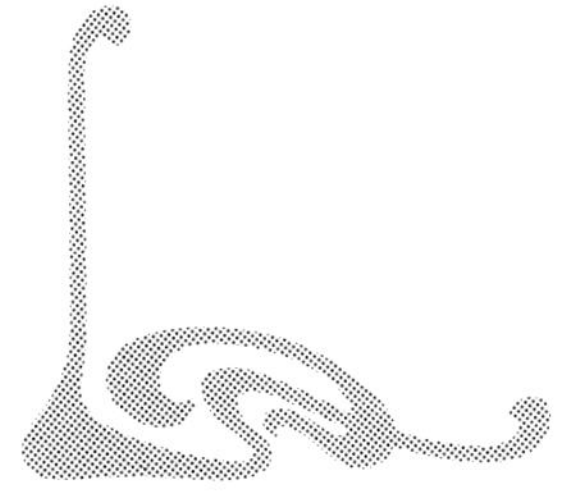

Rudolph Valentino in *The Son of the Sheik* (1926)

Radio
by Rudolph Valentino

Radio of Romance,
        You
Broadcasting to the universe
    All that is most blessed
        In all things,
But to me alone
        The melody of your Love
    Flows through
        The artery
        Of time and Space,
For unity,
    Can never know division

(While unrelated to the motion picture, it seems appropriate to include this verse as a sample of the poems of Rudolph Valentino, which were published under the collective title of Day Dreams *by Macfadden Publications in 1923)*

Movie Mothers
by Alfred Hustwick

Oh, we're the movie mothers
    (That's so)
You must have seen
    (You surely know)
Our very charming daughters
    (They are)
Upon the screen:
    (Each one's a star)
And we're the ones who taught them
    (To act)
All that they know
    (Their poise and tact)
The way they walk and talk
    (We did)
Everything to us they owe
    (That's no kid.)
We're their mothers. . . . .
We protect them,
Pick their stories, and select them
Doting mothers. . . . .
Proper persons to direct them
In the parts they play;
On the job. . . . .
Our only duty
Is to guard each lovely cutie,
Night and day. . . . .
And exploit her youth and beauty
In a business way;
We're their mothers. . . . .
You can't blame us
If at times they fail to claim us,
And no others. . . . .
We're the ones who made them famous
And we'll have our say!
Will ever. . . . .
We can guide them
Ever. . . . .

To our apron-strings, we've tied them
And you'll find us right beside them
Ever. . . . .
When they draw their pay!
Draw their pay!

(reprinted from the program for The Writers' Revue *of 1923)*

It Looks Nice in the Movies
by Baron Ireland

The Sheik, in the film, grabbed his victim
And lugged her away to his tent,
Where his subsequent actions were flagrant infractions
Of every known rule for a gent.
But Saydie, observing him, murmured,
While she blushed to the brim of her hat,
"Well, maybe I'm sappy, but I could die happy
If some guy would treat me like that!"

Later on, when the movie was over,
And Saydie was walking back home,
With deserts dissolving and Arabs revolving
In dizzying whirls through her dome,
A shoe clerk tipped Saydie his kelly,
Attempting her progress to stop.
"Say, beat it!" snapped Saydie, "You bum, I'm a lady,
Go on or I'll yell for a cop!"

(reprinted from Life, *June 14, 1923, page 11)*

Robin Hood in Main Street
(Academy of Music: Douglas Fairbanks)
by T.L.

Speed up, speed up! More speed, more speed! . . .
A knight now vaults upon his steed.

But sooth to say we scarce descry
Whether 'tis Robin or Sir Guy.

Ha, now he has him! . . . Who has whom? . . .
He's down! Who's down? . . .
Quick, quick! A room,

A moat, a throne, a stair, a cell,
A wall, a forest—piled pell-mell—

Mixed up with lances, arms and legs,
Pork chops and pincers, casques and kegs;

And through it all *one* head a-bobbin';
Puck? Peter Pan . . . Why, no—it's Robin!

It is, it was. He's gone again!
And where he stood three score lie slain.

Now, Little John! . . . Why, no—it's Will . . .
I say, who called the Forest *still?*

O ye who thumb the ancient pages,
And seek to see the Middle Ages . . .

Well, Doug, they say, *is* middle-aged,
Yet scarce the Robin that I paged.

These movies move—we all agree.
Alas, they move too quick for me!

(reprinted from Life, *July 12, 1923, page 3)*

Star Dusters

A thing of beauty is Leatrice Joy forever.
People who live in Gaston Glass houses should not throw Lewis Stones.
Colleen Moore the merrier.
Marion Davies and repent at leisure.
Better to have Ben Turpined than never to have Bessie Loved at all.
It's a Lon Chaney that has no turning.
Lois and Behold.
Dorothy Mackaill while the sun shines.
Money Mix the mare go.
It is more blessed to Gish than to receive.

(reprinted from Film Fun, *Vol. XXXVIII, No. 413, September 1923, page 3)*

Where the Western Begins
by Thomas Pye

Where does the Western begin?
Out where the bunk's a little stronger;
Where right is righter and wrong is wronger;
Out where the hokum lingers longer—
That's where the Western begins.

Out in the great wide open lots,
Where no one shrinks from close-up shots
Where men are men and children tots;
Out where a horse is a he-man's pal—
A curious chum for an an-i-mal!—
And the ranch is run by the old man's gal—
That's where the Western begins.

Out where a cowboy's kept aloof
Unless he mounts his horse from the roof—
He drops with a thud, and the horse says "Oof!"—
That's where the Western begins.

Out where emotions surge and spill,
But keep within range of the camera still;
Out where the sheriff shoots to thrill;
Out where mush plays a double-header;
Out where red blood's a little bit redder,
And the sense of humor a whole lot deader—
That's where the Western begins.

(reprinted from Life, *May 21, 1925, page 25)*

Barbara La Marr*
by Margaret E. Sangster

Somewhere, back of the sunset,
Where loveliness never dies—
She dwells in a land of glory,
With dreams in her lifted eyes.

And laughter lives all about her,
And music sways on the air;
She is far from all thought of sadness,
Of passion, and doubt, and care!

The flowers of vanished April,
The lost gold of summer's mirth,
Are wrapped, like a cloak, about her,
Who hurried, too soon, from earth.

And we who have known her splendor—
A beauty that brought swift tears;
Will cherish her vision, always,
To brighten the drifting years!

(reprinted from Photoplay, Vol. XXIX, No. 5, April 1926, page 41)

*Barbara La Marr, who was noted for her beauty, died on January 30, 1926, at the age of 29; her films include *The Prisoner of Zenda* (1922), *The Eternal City* (1923) and *The White Moth* (1924).

Movie Lovers
by Baron Ireland

The lady in the tenth row is much too near,
The lady in the fifth row is too far away.
The lady in the twelth row has quite a good ear.
The lady in the ninth row was marcelled to-day.

The lady on the side aisle can't see a thing.
The lady in the gallery ab*hors* the parterre.
The lady in the loge wishes some one would sing.
The lady in the dress circle's just bobbed her hair.

The lady in the red hat is scented too high.
The lady in the green dress is showing a knee.
That's what you see and that's what you hear.
What's on the program? Well, don't ask *me*!

(reprinted from Life, *May 20, 1926, page 11)*

On Hirsute Flawlessness
by Simonetta

I much adore the realistic touches
As practiced by the more efficient men
In all the better moving pictures, such as
A Woman of Paris, Greed, Kiss Me Again.
I yield applause in honor to each actor
And actress who performs with truth and care;
But here is an objectionable factor:
How is it that they never muss their hair?

The screen flickers. A lady wakes from slumber,
Dismal and unappealing is her room;
I note delightfully the lavish number
Of objects quite veracious in their gloom.
Her nightgown has a torn and trailing border;
She yawns; she has a most untidy air;
And yet her tresses are in perfect order!
How is it that they never muss their hair?

Regard this youth. You've really got to doff your
Chapeau to him for keeping so intact
The glory of his scintillating coiffure
In spite of all the villains he has whacked.
Long and unceasingly the man has scuffled,
Bitter and fierce has been the eyes' wild glare,
But still his hair is utterly unruffled.
How is it that they never muss their hair?

(reprinted from Life, *May 20, 1926, page 12)*

What Makes the Pictures?
by George F. Magoffin

"It's money makes the pictures," said the august powers that be,
"So we'll spend six million dollars and we'll see what we shall see;
"It's money gives us prestige, spins the world 'round like a top."
So they spent six million dollars—and the picture was a flop.

Can money make a picture that will make the heart-strings crack,
Control our wilful fancies, and send them speeding back
Along the dark'ning ghost-trails of our moldering mistakes,
To rescue from oblivion some joy its magic wakes?

Can money make a picture that will wake some primal chord,
Deep buried in conventions, but vibrant as the sword
That leaps to battle action in response to savage will,
Exultant in its freedom, and the lust to maim and kill?

Can money make a picture that will make the tear drops start
In sympathetic feeling with some human interest part,
Some self-effacing action that asks not why nor when,
But only seeks the privilege of making whole again?

Can money make a picture? Has insensate gold the art
To simulate the passions of the pulsing human heart,
To evoke a fellow-feeling through emotions' subtle sway
'Till we forget the action is just a picture play?

No! "The play's the thing!" said Shakespeare. Keep your eye upon the gun,
For not by crass abstractions can victory be won.
"Hold the mirror up to nature, wherein each must play a part";
Not money makes the pictures—but the understanding heart.

(reprinted from The Film Spectator, *Vol. III, No. 1, March 5, 1927, page 2)*

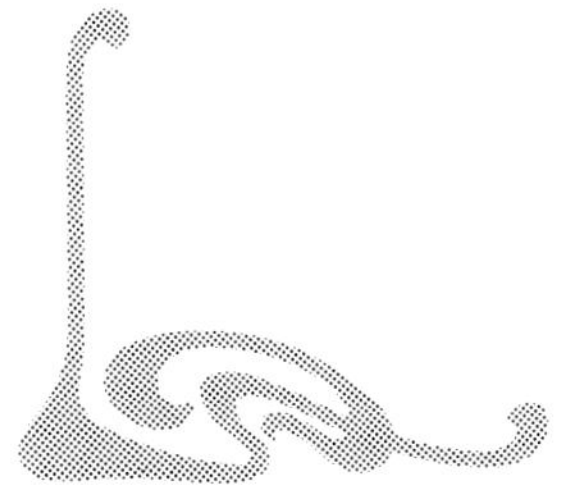

Stars Who Never Were—
by Margaret E. Sangster

The great stars come, the great stars go,
Some like a sunset, with a slow,
Rare spread of color and of light;
Some like a comet in the night.
The great stars dawn and die—some pass
Like dim shapes in a looking glass.
And some there are who laugh and stay,
Because the public smiles their way!

But what about the ones who peer
Around the corner of each year,
With hopes half old, and yet half new—
With dreams that never dare come true?
The ones who wait life's great romance—
Spelled out for them in this word—"Chance!"
The ones who never feel the stir
Of fame—*the stars who never were?*

This girl who glances from the mob,
This boy whose pulses feel the throb
Of keen ambition—this wan face,
This body, with a dancer's grace . . .
What of the ones who work and strive,
Yet never, never can arrive?
What of the weary souls that wait,
While genius turns to fear and hate?

The extras—eyes and legs and lips,
No more! They fade and wonder slips
Beyond their reach, while others take
Life's fullness . . But though hearts may break,
They struggle on, past pain and loss,
Although their goal may be a cross—
The gallant ones that never win,
The stars—the stars that might have been!

(reprinted from Photoplay, *Vol. XXXII, No. 1, June 1927, page 63)*

Projector
by Hilda Doolittle

Light takes new attribute
and yet his old
glory
enchants;
not this,
not this, they say,
lord as he was of the heiratic dance,
of poetry
and majesty
and pomp,
master of shrines and gateways
and of doors,
of markets
and the cross-road
and the street;
not this,
they say;
but we say otherwise
and greet
light
in new attribute,
insidious fire;
light reasserts
his power
reclaims the lost;
in a new blaze of splendour
calls the host
to reassemble
and to readjust
all severings
and differings of thought,
all strife and strident bickering
and rest;
O fair and blest,
he strides forth young and pitiful and strong,
a king of blazing splendour and of gold,
and all the evil
and the tyrannous wrong
that beauty suffered

finds its champion,
light
who is god
and song.

He left the place they built him
and the halls,
he strode so simply forth,
they knew him not;
no man deceived him,
no,
nor ever will,
with meagre counterfeit
of ancient rite,
he knows all hearts
and all imagining
of plot
and counterplot
and mimicry,
this measure of beauty with a rod,
no formula
could hold him
and no threat
recall him
who is god.

Yet he returns,
O unrecorded grace,
over
and under
and through us
and about;
the stage is set now
for his mighty rays;
light,
light that batters gloom,
the Pythian
lifts up a fair head
in a lowly place,
he shows his splendour
in a little room;
he says to us,
be glad

and laugh,
be gay;
I have returned
though in an evil day
you crouched despairingly
who had no shrine;
we had no temple and no temple fire
for all these said
and mouthed
and said again;
beauty is an endighter
and is power
of city
and of soldiery
and might,
beauty is city
and the state
and dour duty,
beauty is this and this and this dull thing,
forgetting who was king.

Yet still he moves
alert,
invidious,
this serpent creeping
and this shaft of light,
his arrows slay
and still his foot-steps
dart
gold
in the market place;
vision returns
and with new vision
fresh
hope
to the impotent;
tired feet that never knew a hill-slope
tread
fabulous mountain sides;
worn
dusty feet
sink in soft drift of pine
needles

and anodyne
of balm and fir and myrtle-trees
and cones
drift across weary brows
and the sea-foam
marks the sea-path
where no sea ever comes;
islands arise where never islands were,
crowned with the sacred palm
or odorous cedar;
waves sparkle and delight
the weary eyes
that never saw the sun fall in the sea
nor the bright Pleaiads rise.

(*reprinted from* Close Up, *No. 1, July 1927, pages 46–51*)

Chaney's Latest

Lon Chaney will star in
"The Wandering Jew,"
All Hollywood tells us
The Story is true.

He's given us gangsters,
And skeletons white,
He's given us monsters,
To fill us with fright—

He's given us robbers,
And given us freaks,
He's broken his body,
And puffed out his cheeks.

Oh, he's been a hunchback,
He's been without legs;
His arms have been stumps,
And his feet have been pegs.

He's been a gorilla,
A museum piece,
He's said it with crutches,
And false teeth and grease.

And so, as a climax,
As something quite new—
They've handed him this one,
"The Wandering Jew"—

He's done men from China,
He's done a Marine,
But now, as his latest . . .
*(Why bring in Levine?)**

(reprinted from Photoplay, *Vol. XXXIII, No. 3, August 1927, page 38)*

**Lon Chaney never did make a film version of The Wandering Jew.*

Emil Jannings as August Shilling in *The Way of All Flesh*

Drooping, heavy, careworn body,
Hands that hang at either side;
Clothes a little worn and shoddy,
Eyes that gleam with gentle pride.
Shoulders that can show emotion,
As no other shoulders do—
Genius, from across the ocean,
Making tarnished dreams come true.

Tragedy—not glaring, shrieking,
But the groping sort we know;
Tenderness, tongue-tied, but speaking,
In each smile that dares to glow!
Humbleness and faith that reaches
To all hearts that living teaches.

(reprinted from Photoplay, *Vol. XXXII, No. 3, August 1927, page 38)*

A Tribute——Robert McKim 1887–1927*

He played so many villains on the screen,
He sneered so often in the hero's face,
That we had set him down to film disgrace,
To being "most unkind" and "very mean!"

And yet he was a prey to circumstances,
He started as a villain—and, no doubt,
He often vainly longed to turn about,
To play the lead in pretty, light romances!

We like to think that he is smiling now,
That all the parts he plays are pleasant roles,
That deal with happy hearts and joyous souls.
That he is always called to take a bow!

And, at his passing, may the world recall,
That he, in ugly places, never shirked,
That honestly he lived and played and worked,
And was the meanest villain of them all!

(reprinted from Photoplay, Vol. XXXII, No. 3, August 1927, page 38)

*Among McKim's many films are *The Mark of Zorro* (1920), *The Spoilers* (1924) and *The Bat* (1926).

7th Heaven[*]
by George F. Magoffin

The picture, somehow, was delightfully different,
Some subtle effluence beguiling the sense
As the fragrance of meadows or ploughed fields or lilacs
Conjures fond recollections of Life's super moments,
When the rose-glow of happiness softly about us
Enfolds us with intricate gossamer weavings
Whose motif is love and whose charm is illusion.

So, the picture engendered an aura supernal
Which enfolded the sense with its magical charm,
Each sequence in tempo a smooth-flowing river
That whispered the folk-lore of forest and plain;
Through sunshine and shadow on this stream we swept onward,
And thrilled with each triumph and wept with each pain.

We forgot that the play was a mere motion picture;
Genius alone has such artistry true.
Time paused, that each gesture, each nuance, revealing,
Be accorded the homage so justly its due.

We saw not alone with our eyes; our feelings
Augmented each sequence from Memory's store;
We perceived with the heart; its lucid revealings
Affirming our kinship with lives lived before.

And thus did the soul born of this lucid picture
Run Emotion's wide gamut from laughter to tears.
The illusions we cherish! Does maturity lose them?
No! The soul of this picture quite vanquished our fears.

(reprinted from The Film Spectator, *Vol. IV, No. 6, November 12, 1927, page 3)*

7th Heaven was released by William Fox in 1927; it starred Janet Gaynor and Charles Farrell and was directed
by Frank Borzage.

The Film
by Clarence E. Flynn

The film clicks on. Life moves apace,
The autumn takes the place of spring.
Time writes his story on each face,
Change works his will with everything.
There is no pause at Beauty's bower,
No waiting where the roses grow,
Not for a single sunny house.
On ever does the story go.

The film clicks on. The sun dips low.
Deepens the plot through which we move.
The pathway shortens. Onward go
The feet of hope and toil and love.
But one by one do things come right,
The powers of darkness reel and fall,
The passing clouds give place to light
And gladness conquers after all.

(reprinted from Moving Picture Stories, *Vol. XXX, No. 777, November 15, 1927, page 22)*

Charles Chaplin directing *The Circus* (1928)

Charlie Chaplin in the Leading Role of *The Circus*

With all the pathos, all the wistful yearning
Of broken dreams behind a Pierrot mask—
With all the genius that is ever burning
Within his soul, he hurries to the task
Of making people smile whose souls were weary,
Of making people laugh whose hopes were dead. . . .
There is something that is more than cheery
In every gesture of his hand, his head.

The calling of the sawdust ring, the wonder
Of high trapeze and riding and romance,
The tinsel—and the heart-break that lies under
The tanbark floor on which the troupers dance.
Oh, he has caught them all—the joy, the pain—
And brought them close, to make us young again!

(reprinted from Photoplay, *Vol. XXXIII, No. 2, January 1928, page 63)*

Emil Jannings as Sergius Alexander in *The Last Command*

Against the melodrama of the story,
He stands—a figure tragic, brave and bold—
He never seems to lose his look of glory,
Though beaten by the world, and growing old.
He who had known the flame of pomp and power,
He who had scorned the cringing and the weak,
Could never wholly bow beneath the shower
Of scorn and poverty and words men speak.

The studio has made a screen behind him
Of shadow shapes that only come and go;
He is no shadow, we will always find him,
Where blood is hot, and passions dare to glow.
Pathetic? Yes, perhaps, we watch through tears,
As he goes marching down the broken years!

(reprinted from Photoplay, *Vol. XXXIII, No. 4, March 1928, page 58)*

When Night-Time Comes—
by Margaret E. Sangster

When night-time comes to Hollywood,
I think the lady moon looks down,
With kindliness and sympathy,
Upon the silent, resting town.

She, gently swaying in the sky,
Bathes with a healing, silver fire,
The tired city that has wept,
And laughed, and worked, and known desire!

And all the faiths that have been lost,
And all the plans that went awry,
Are giving back to dreaming hearts
Her benediction from the sky.

For, as the wistful breezes sing,
And as the clouds about her creep,
The lady moon is keeping guard
Above the earth-bound stars who sleep.

(reprinted from Photoplay, *Vol. XXXIII, No. 4, March 1928, page 59)*

"TALKIES"
by Welford Beaton

The moving picture speaks,
And having spoken,
The silence that one seeks
In films is broken.
Alas for those fair faces
Whose beguilance
Lay in their thousand graces—
And their silence.

(reprinted from The Film Spectator, *Vol. VII, No. 2, January 5, 1929, page 15)*

Fade-Out
by A.S.C.

Twinkle, twinkle, movie star,
In your fancy motor car:
When the talkies make the grade
You will be a chambermaid.

(reprinted from Life, *January 11, 1929, page 4)*

The Technique of the Sound Accompaniment
by R.C. O'Brien

He meets her, and it is June;
Then somebody sings the theme song;
They both fall in love quite soon;
Then somebody sings the theme song;
But her old man (he is funny),
Thinks the youth just wants his money;
So the youth says: "Goodbye, Honey."
Then somebody sings the theme song.

But she follows him—like that;
Then somebody sings the theme song;
They live in a walkup flat;
While somebody sings the theme song;
They can't live on what he makes;
Soon her hubby she forsakes;
But, without him, her heart aches;
Then somebody sings the theme song.

Comes the War, both grim and gory;
War tunes mingle with the theme song;
He enlists to fight for glory;
Drum beats almost drown the theme song;
He comes home quite celebrated;
He is wined and dined and feted;
Through it all, why, she has waited;
As somebody sings the theme song.

Her old man no longer hollers;
When somebody sings the theme song;
He gives both a million dollars;
Then somebody sings the theme song;
With her parent's change of heart,
They both have a brand new start,
As the movie fans depart
Everybody sings the theme song.

(reprinted from Life, April 5, 1929, page 8)

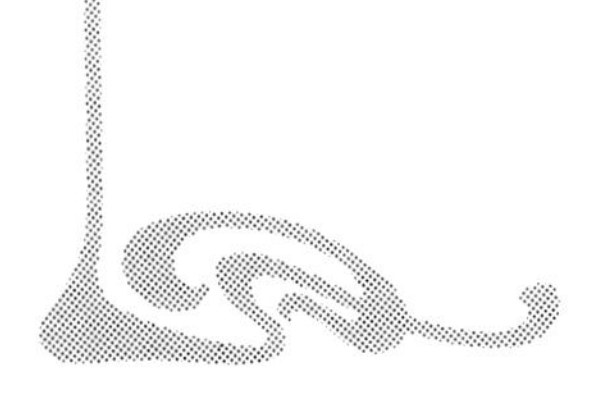

That Magic Picture-Curtain of Sound

When I was little, I used to say
To my lonely self day after day,
"There's a door been closed by God somewhere
Up in the mansions above the air,
And it's shut out the music of life for me."
The chirping of birds, the drip of the sea,
The song of the wind and all lullabies
That soothe the sorrows of heavy eyes—
These were the things they described to me,
Who never had heard a tune or a key.

But now there's a place I can always go,
And there I can almost hear and know
The melodies that they tell about;
For all of a sudden my soul drifts out
Beyond the realm of tangible things;
I hear the sighing of countless wings—
Those ever-fanning pinions of white,
That gloss with silver the darkest night.
Lo! that is not all, for as I wait
Before that snowy curtain of fate
I hear the secrets that lovers tell—
And I keep that music and con it well.
And somehow I fancy that mighty door
That God closed on me forevermore,
Has at last swung open and let me in,
For an instant, to be as I might have been!
And all the day I imagine—
I dream of a phantom cadence strong;
And I catch the matchless, eternal strain
of angels harping heaven's refrain.

O wonder curtain! O master brain
That pierced the depths where my soul has lain!
O Christly pity that let me pass
To the other side of the looking-glass!

Ah, blessings on the genius that woke
Melody from a word unspoke!
Thrice blessings on you who for me found
That magic picture-curtain of sound!

*(reprinted from an editorial by James R. Quirk in which he noted that the passing of the silent film was a genuine
tragedy to the deaf, in* Photoplay, *Vol. XXXVI, No. 1, June 1929, page 30)*

Talkie Love
by Leonard Hall

Now that love has made us wise,
Darling, let us synchronize!

Contract for a happy doom
In a churchly mixing room—

Speak our lines in solemn tone,
To some reverend microphone—

With a special Berlin score
Pledge our love forevermore!

Thus, "in sink," we two shall be
One sound-track through eternity!

(reprinted from Photoplay, *Vol. XXXVI, No. 4, September 1929, page 70)*

The Theme Song of Theme Songwriters
Lyric by Joe Seitman, Music by George Green (By Green with X-Seitman-t)

Verse (with feeling and remorse)
Oh, Mister Producers, please lend us a hear,
We theme song inducers make your pictures dear.
You hand us a plot and we land you a spot,
With a song that will long be remember'd a lot.
But the sweetest music aflow, that we know,
Is the melody render'd with dough.

(Go into Chorus—with a checkbook)
For the theme song of theme songwriters
Is just "A loan at last" (theme song of Morris Plan)
We write jazz and operas and open your eyes.
Say we stop at nothing; we're clever, we guys.
And if you want "Rosie O'Grady" we'll write her right away,
Or "Sweet Auld Lang Syne" that's all in our line.
We write them—that is, if you pay,
But theme songs may come and theme songs may go,
But this theme song always remains:
Without all your checks, we'd hang by our necks, "Awringin' in the Rain."

(reprinted from Rob Wagner's Script, *April 26, 1930, page 8)*

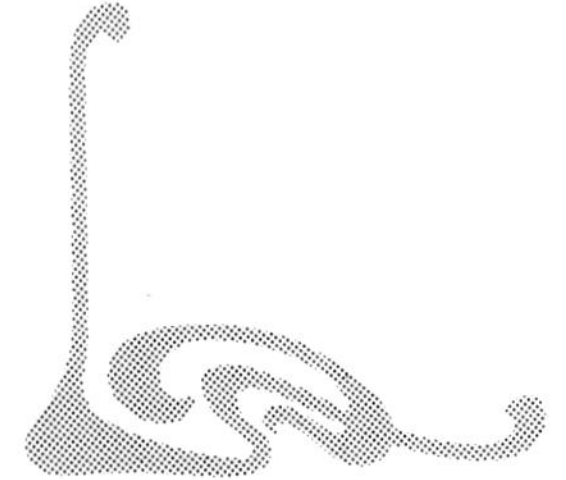

Mabel Normand*
by Margaret E. Sangster

Beneath the gallant sparkle of her laughter,
There always lay the hint of wistfulness,
As if she knew that storm must follow after
The brightest day . . . Perhaps her soul could guess
That tragedy was waiting, eager handed,
To block her path, to stay her dancing feet,
To leave her lonely, pitiful, and stranded . . .
Yet who shall say her life was incomplete?

For, oh, she brought swift smiles to sorry faces
She taught a weary-hearted world to sing;
Her presence lent new grace to lonely places,
She had the radiance of waking spring.
Behind her mask of comedy, she waited
For every hurt the future held in store;
She gave herself to all, nor hesitated . . .
And died when she, at last, could give no more!

(reprinted from Photoplay, *Vol. XXXVII, No. 6, May 1930, page 36)*

*Mabel Normand, the best known of silent screen comediennes, died on February 23, 1930, at the age of 35.

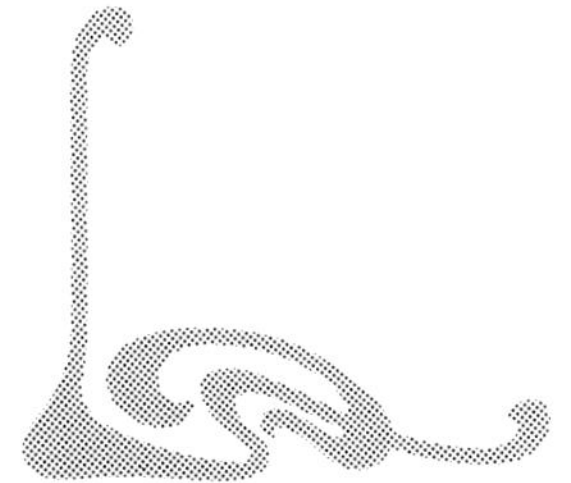

Bigger and Better Publicity
by Parke Cummings

Talkie star breeds wolves as hobby,
Actress weds in hotel lobby,
Star has jumping bean collection,
Star buys yacht in one-ton sections,
Star a record hammer-thrower,
Star was once a doily sewer,
Star shears llamas for diversion,
Star speaks Sanskrit, Dutch and Persian,
Star was once a flag-pole sitter,
Star carves bust from apple fritter,
Star spends week-ends reading Plato,
Crosses eggplant with tomato,
Star makes hole-in-one left handed,
Star gets eight-ton tarpon landed,
Star got start as snowshoe weaver,
Always shaves with butcher's cleaver,
Star a famous yo yo spinner,
Star eats only snails for dinner,
Star shoots hornets with a rifle,
Says the feat is just a trifle,
Star takes bath in sherry cobbler,
Star wins prize with turkey gobbler,
Star gets pleasure kidding Babbitts,
Star keeps healthy racing rabbits,
—Let's hear all their damn-fool habits.

(reprinted from Life, *July 18, 1930, page 18)*

Cinema
(with apologies to Ernest Dowson)
by Norman R. Jaffray

Last night, ah, yesternight, upon the silver screen
There fell thy shadow, Cinema! complete with sound:
The dullest talking picture I had ever seen;
And I was desolate and sick of its cheap passion,
Yea, I was desolate, but kept my ground:
I have been faithful to thee, Cinema, in my fashion

All night (or so it seemed) I watched the tale unreel
Of two anemic brats for whom I did not care,
Faking a puppy-love they did not seem to feel,
And I was desolate and sick of movie passion
When I awoke and found the theater bare:
I have been faithful to thee, Cinema, in my fashion.

They cried for madder music and for a stronger wine:
Flung roses, orchids, riotously with the throng,
Dressed in a style that is not yours or mine;
And I was desolate and bored with all their passion—
Yea, bored to death; but though the show was long,
I have been faithful to thee, Cinema, in my fashion.

But faithfulness is hard, when on the silver-sheet
Such guff as this is shown: an adolescent clown
Pretending love for some blonde cutie sickish-sweet,
So I am desolate, and quite fed up with passion;
And the next Cinema that comes to town
Will find me faithless to it, in no uncertain fashion

(reprinted from Life, *May 1, 1931, page 13)*

Valentine for Louella Parsons
by Betty Fisher

Dear L.O.P., it seems to me,
You're full of perspicuity,
I never saw one so astute,
In getting to the very root
Of movie folks' perplexities,
(which saturate their hides like fleas)
Why, it's uncanny, absolutely,
To hear you utter resolutely,
That, "so and so—the chuckle-monger,
Ain't 'that way' 'bout his wife no longer,"
And yet, a scribe's proclivities,
Are not confined to such as these,
With open ears and nimble hoof,
You skylark on the Roosevelt Roof,
And if your rhumba grows intense,
We know you've spotted more events
Called "blessed" in your daily column,
Louella, HOW can you keep solemn!

(reprinted from Rob Wagner's Script, *February 11, 1933, page 2)*

Had I Made Claudette
by "The Playboy"

If I were God I wouldn't care,
Had I but made Claudette Colbert,
How mundane things had gone awry
Elsewhere beneath the envious sky,
For I would know there couldn't be
A better job than that, you see,
And that I'd made a perfect score
For once, howe'er I'd failed before.

On things askew in other ways
I'd turn a calm, forgiving gaze;
I'd let "hard times" go hang, and war
Could chase itself to Hades, for,
With sweet Claudette upon my mind,
To aught but beauty I'd be blind,
And I should feel assured that she
Would change the whole wide world for me.

I'd find that every flower that grew
Reflected my contentment, too,
And every bird on flaunting wing
Had learned to soar and sweetly sing.
In fact, if I had made Claudette
I doubt if I'd have one regret
For all my failures of the past;
For here were real success, at last!

(reprinted from Rob Wagner's Script, *February 11, 1933, page 3)*

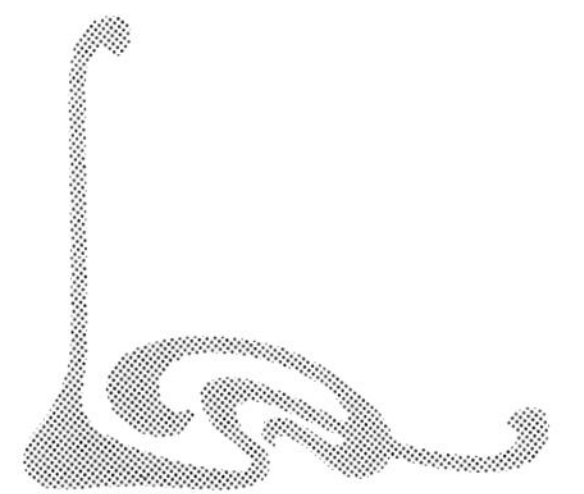

Mother Goose Goes Hollywood
by Robert Watson

Mary had a little ham
Along with eggs for tea,
She went to bed and in her dreams
Some funny things did see.
She saw a "humble" female star,
A "modest" leading man,
A perfect play, so well produced,
It never left the can!

The producer in his "sanctum"
Was counting out his money.
The "star" was in his bathing suit
Canoodling his honey.
The chorine in the dressing room
Was taking off her clothes
When by came a "Big Bad Wolf"
and *what* do you suppose?

The King of Hearts
He met some tarts
All in their night array.
The Queen of Hearts
She found those tarts
And sent them all away.
The King of Hearts
Called for his tarts,
But at their bedroom door
He turned and fled
Straight back to bed.
—He knew his Queenie's snore!

Fe, Fi, Fo Fum,
O, for the voice of an Englishmun!
Be he living, or be he dead,
I'll steal his accent to make my bread.

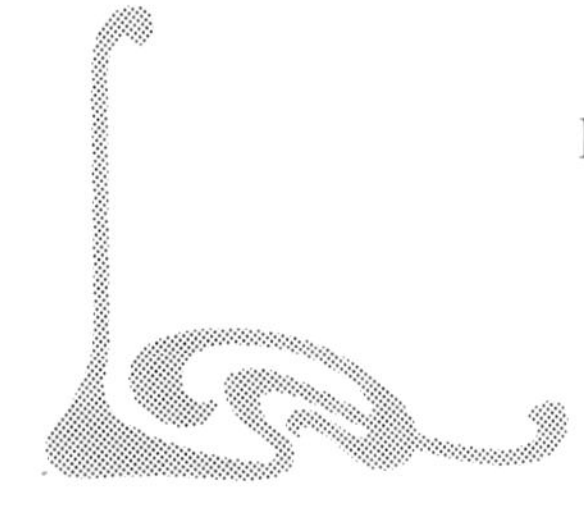

Went old Mrs. Grundy
To borrow, last Monday,
Because her old "undies" were done.
But when she got there
Her "prospect" was bare,
And so Mrs. Grundy got none.

Twinkle, twinkle, little Star;
No one wonders who you are.
All your secrets have been told
In box office chase for gold.

There was a Producer, who lived in a stew,
He had so many relatives he didn't know what to do,
So he gave them some jobs without any dough,
And soon they departed—and so did his woe.

Pat-a-cake, pat-a-cake, studio-man,
Make us a picture as fast as you can.
Pad it, and twist it—the old theme will do;
Picture-fans never need anything new.

(reprinted from Rob Wagner's Script, *July 14, 1934, page 3)*

Every Other Place
by Gouverneur Morris

You who look down on Hollywood
And you who frown on Hollywood,
Have you at home in your own towns
More satisfactory ups and downs?

We hold no brief for Hollywood,
Nor saint nor thief in Hollywood.
The sinners and the virtuous
Are so much applesauce to us.

With tongue in cheek view Hollywood,
Unbiased peek at Hollywood,
Dwell without shame in Hollywood
And play the game in Hollywood.

Good luck, bad luck, virtue, vice
Pleasant things and things not nice
Rackets, snatches, falls from grace,
Ecstasy and grief and moan
Spell not Hollywood alone—
They spell every other place!

(reprinted from The Screen Guilds' Magazine, *August 1934, page 17)*

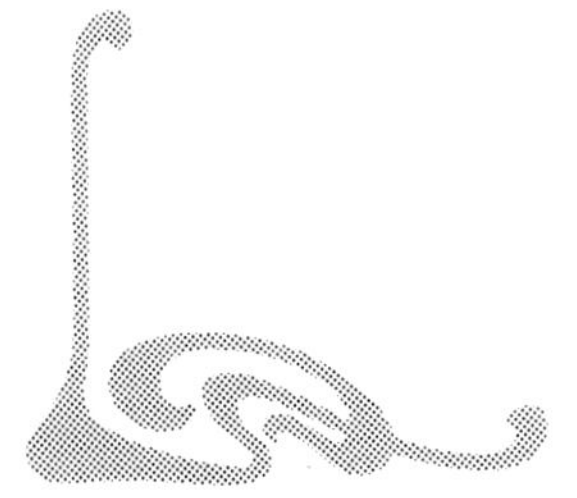

Leading Man
by Leslie Curtis

If Claudette Colbert glanced my way
I'd label it a gala day
But if Kay Francis sought me, too,
I wouldn't know just what to do.
Unless by some kind act of God
My arms could circle Thelma Todd.
But I would leave them all and run
To play a part with Irene Dunne.

(reprinted from Rob Wagner's Script, *September 1, 1934, page 5)*

The Celestial Cinema
by Frank Morgan*

When Metro's last picture is finished,
And the film is twisted and dried
And the oldest Western has faded
And the youngest Disney has died
We shall rest (and faith we shall need it!)
Lie down for an aeon or two
Till another Louiebee Mayer
Shall bid us to work anew.
And those that were good shall be featured
They shall have their names on a chair
And someone to hold them a mirror
And someone to brush their hair,
And only L.B. shall praise us
And only L.B. shall blame
And no one shall work for money
And no one shall work for fame
But each for the joy of working
In a part that is heaven sent,
Shall play the part as he sees it
For an agent's ten per cent.

(reprinted from Rob Wagner's Script, *October 13, 1934, page 3)*

*Character actor Frank Morgan (1890–1949) is best remembered for his portrayal of the title role in *The Wizard of Oz* (1939).

The Last Laugh!
by Robert Charles Rothafel

"Hit 'em!
Quiet!
They're turning—
Speed!"
Kleig Lights—
Hooded Cameras—
Sound Mikes—
Technicians—
Sweating—
Grim Faced.
Action. . . .
"Laugh everybody.
We're payin'
Ya dough!
This
Damned scene
Is funny.
Say,
You dames—
Second row—
This
Is supposed
To be
COMEDY—
Not Draaaama!"

"Cut it!
Cut!
Cut!
N.G.
For sound,"
Said
The bespectacled Mixer
From his
Sanctum Sanctorum,
"Not enough laughter,
Come on,
Let's try again . . ."
"Hit 'em!

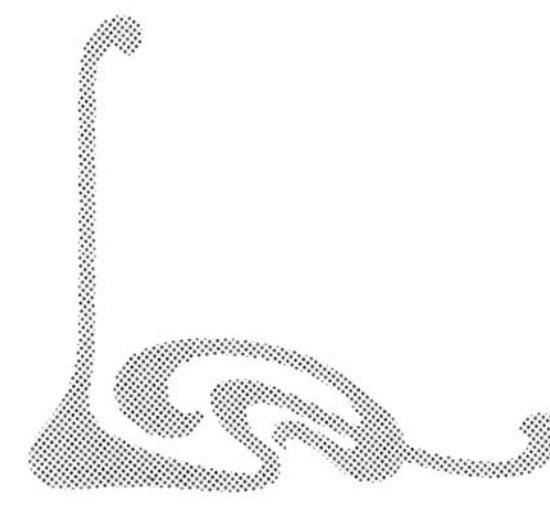

Quiet, please,
They're turning—
Speed!"
Kleig Lights—
Hooded Cameras—
Sound Mikes—
Technicians,
Sweating—
Grim faced.

Sync,
Action. . . .
"Laugh!
Laugh!"

But again
There greeted
This strident
Voice,
Nothing
But
Weird Sounds—
Mirthless Cackling . . .
Unintelligible
Unintelligent.
"Laugh!
Laugh!
Hey you—
In the fourth row—
Can't you laugh
Any better
Than that?"
Two hundred hearts
Stood still . . .

"Cut it!
Cut!"
Four hundred ears
Heard
The hysterical screams
Of a woman
Who revolted
For the last time.
"I'll laugh!—

I'll laugh!"
And
With a terrifying shriek
She dropped dead
At their feet—
From hunger,
Exposure
And . . . laughter.

"N.G.
For Sound,"
Said
The bespectacled Mixer
From his
Sanctum Sanctorum,
"Ready—
Another take!"
"Close in, everybody—
Fill up
That empty gap. . . .
Okaaay.
Hit 'em!
Quiet!
They're turning—
Speed!"
Kleig Lights—
Hooded Cameras—
Sound Mikes—
Technicians,
Sweating—
Grim faced.

Sync,
Action. . . .
"Laugh everybody
For Christ's Sakes
Laugh!"

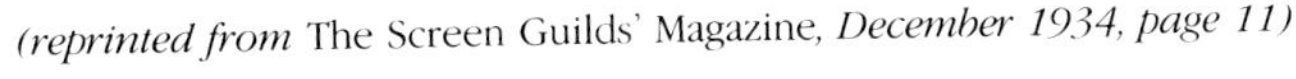

(reprinted from The Screen Guilds' Magazine, *December 1934, page 11)*

Lo! The Poor Extra
by Mason E. Litson

At the Studio Gate where the hopeful wait
Stood an extra man, forlorn.
His heart was sad, his soles were bad
And his blue serge suit looked worn.
He had waited there with expectant air
For a lucky "replacement" call
Till the clock said nine, and the waiting line
Was given the word "That's all!"

He was not as loud as the motley crowd
Who were voicing their various kicks.
And he lit a "cig" that was not as big
As it was when he came at six.
Then he heard his name as a vision came
Clad in "knickers" of gaudy hue;
It was Lucky Case, the "yessing ace"
Of director Bill McCue.

His heart went light as a "ducat" white
Was placed in his eager hand
With instructions short to at once report
As a native of some far land.
Where the balmy air of a climate rare
Knows no Winter, Spring or Fall
And a tropic sun makes it just good fun
To wear no clothes at all.

This meant of course that he would, perforce,
Be required to don a coat
That had been designed by a master mind
To capture an extra's "goat."
Not made or planned by a tailor's hand
Though it fitted him everywhere,
It was "body-paint" and its putrid taint
Was almost too much to bear.

From a filthy can, this coat of tan
Was generously applied
With a mangy brush and a careless rush
Till it covered his own pale hide.
It was some relief that a "gee-string," brief,
Was part of his strange costume;
But his gait belied his native pride
As he slunk from the "make-up" room.

The "set" that day, I must stop to say,
Was a jungle, where everyone knows
There are vines and weeds and a thing that feeds
On blood, through a long sharp nose.
There's a sun that's hot; and a shady spot
Where chills rack a naked frame.
There are fallen trees and flies and bees
And things that I need not name.

In this tropic glade, the Extra played
Through a merciless summer day;
But he "stood the gaff" and tried to laugh
As he thought of his liberal (?) pay.
That check for ten good "iron men"
He'd figured out to a dime;
So the bites and stings and other things
Only served to pass the time.

As dusk drew nigh in the evening sky,
He was cheered by the happy thought
That the day was done; and he soon would run
To the joys that his toil had bought.
He was wrong again and a look of pain
With maybe a touch of hate
Came over his face as Lucky Case
said "eat!—and be back at eight."

In a coat of paint and a "gee-string" quaint,
He couldn't go "off the lot";
And the lunch-room there had a bill-of-fare
That was C.O.D. "to the dot."
So he nursed his gloom in the Extra Room
For an hour which seemed like four.
Till the "ace's pet" called "ON THE SET!"
And the grind began once more.

Through the long, long night; in a blaze of light
That shrivelled each painted pore,
He came and went with a mind intent
On the onerous coat he wore.
But the dawn at last swept the horrid past
Aside, like a vanquished foe.
He forgot the "paint" and the "gee-string," quaint,
As he hurried to get his "dough."

With clothes half on and a visage wan,
He stood 'neath the cashier's frown;
And the "ducat" white clutched hard and tight
In a hand still painted brown.
On that fatal morn it had been drawn
For someone who didn't arrive;
And the sum it paid (so the cashier said)
Wasn't "ten," but a measly "five."

Two days well done for the price of one
Had taxed him a bit too far;
And his jaw was tense as he started thence
To where he had parked his "car."
The straw that cracks the camels' backs
Now smote him across the spine.
For the ticket he saw on the coupe door
Meant a five-dollar parking fine.

(reprinted from The Screen Guilds' Magazine, *May 1935, page 20)*

Unsung Heroes
by Ralph Birchard

We've fought with Clive in India,
We've ranged the Spanish Main,
We've battled with the Rooshians and the Turks
We landed at Gallipoli,
We bumped 'em off in Tripoli,
We helped to give some Bedouins the works.

We've licked our weight in Irish,
We've been up against the Japs,
We've drunk our way from Singapore to Nome.
We have walked knee-deep in blood,
Which we much prefer to mud,
There ain't no place where we ain't been known to roam.

We have joined with the Crusades—
Taken part in Morgan's raids—
We have whopped it up for Caesar and for Bruce.
We have died a thousand deaths
And endured some trenchant breaths.
In the wars we fight there's no such thing as truce.

On our tough and sinewy rumps
We have taken plenty bumps
Putting pep into some pretty pallid plots.
We have sacrificed our lives
Facing murderous seventy-fives—
And we've never had to venture off the lots.

(reprinted from Rob Wagner's Script, *June 22, 1935, page 3)*

Oh Mr. Laemmle
by Preston Sturges

Oh Mr. Laemmle,
How's all the femily?
All those boys, all those girls, all those brains?
Your pictures seem to say:
"We were made in that old-fashioned family way."

But was it too menly
To fire Stenly?
After all those nice kids he made.
Deent you realize a boy with so much heart,
Could knock you off a relative for every part?

(Found in the Preston Sturges files at UCLA; obviously written after Stanley Bergerman, Laemmle's son-in-law, was dismissed in late 1935)

Movie Makers
by Berton Braley

Directors of the Cinema I sing!
(And if the stanzas lack a lyric swing
And all the rhyming stuff that I rehearse
Is doggerel that goes from bad to verse,
Excuse it, please! And kindly blame the crime
Upon the editor, who ordered rhyme!)
The Muse will now proceed to do her stuff
And if the Muse amuses, that's enough.

Cecil B. DeMille

A film directed by DeMille
Fills all the eyes there are to fill
With palaces, palladiums
And baths the size of stadiums.
When super-films grow bigger still
They'll be directed by DeMille.
Gargantua's direct apostle,
DeMille's Tremendous, Vast, Colossal!

Ernst Lubitsch

Ernst Lubitsch, whose delicate touch,
Fills pictures with sparkle and such
Was born in Berlin (where they do not go in
For lightness and humor so much!)
But Ernst has been happily blest
With quite un-Teutonian zest
("One Hour with You" and "Desire" are two
Which illustrate Ernst at his best!)

Mervyn LeRoy

To Mervyn LeRoy
I hereby offer an "Attaboy!"
For "Five Star Final" and "Anthony Adverse"
(Excuse me if I have to design all this in Ogden Nash's type of mad verse,
And to write lines as long and complicated as these are
In order to mention that Mervyn LeRoy made Oil for the Lamps of
China and Little Caesar,
Which are among the many fine pictures in which Warner Brothers employ
The brilliant directional abilities of Mervyn LeRoy!)

George Cukor

You could fill up a sizable book, or
A catalogue, naming the cast
Of actors directed by Cukor
The stars of the present and past,
Jeanne Eagels, the Barrymores, Rambeau
And Howard and Shearer and Landi,
(For Cukor we'd light up a flambeau if only a flambeau were handy!)

Frank Capra

I've a General Yen for the work that's Capra-cious
And I'm saying again that his wit is delicious
You can count with delight on the hits he will score
For "It Happened One Night"—and will happen some more!

Rouben Mamoulian

It's hard to speak coolly in
Presenting R. Mamoulian,
Whose cerebrial ability
Reveals such versatility.
There's magic of the genie in
The work of this Armenian.

Irving G. Thalberg

Irving G.
Thalberg, he
Said to himself, "I am going to be
Somebody BIG in the movies—and stars will take orders from me!"
Irving G.
Thalberg, he
Rose to the heights where he'd figured to be.
Stars took his orders and he did it with vim
(He married Miss Shearer, but probably SHE
doesn't take orders from him!)

Alfred E. Green

"Disraeli" made George Arliss—and Al Green made Disraeli,
A feature which made owners rich
And clicked the turnstyles gaily;
"Green Goddess," "Golden Arrow," "Colleen"—The Talking Screen
Was pie—with sauce, to this old boss
Of "Silents"—Alfred Green!

Darryl F. Zanuck

Darryl F. Zanuck—The name rhymes with "bannock"—
(That's Scotch for—I do not know what!)
From Wahoo, Nebraska (which rhymes with "Alaska")
First got on a Hollywood lot
As story-concocter, Scenario-Doctor
And probably Gag-Man as well,
But now his constructions of super-productions
Are constantly "ringing the bell!"

Erich von Stroheim

Von Stroheim and his monocle deserve a lengthy chronicle,
(To genius from Vienna I should pen a Book a week)
But I must be laconical and say "Behind that monocle
A brilliant mind is lurking—and it's working
Like a streak!"

John Ford

We'll name "The Informer," John Ford,
As one of the hits you have scored
And then there's "Judge Priest"
Which has never quite ceased
To make our hearts warmer, John Ford.
(And the "Lost Patrol" can't be ignored, John Ford!)

Walter Wanger

Follow "The Trail of the Lonesome Pine"
And your life, which was growing duller,
Begins to glow and to rise and shine
With the glory of Technicolor.
As the Wanger magic and necromancy
Beckon you on through the land of fancy.

James Cruze

And now let's fill a brimming flagon
Clear to the brim, and drink the same
To Jimmy Cruze, whose "Covered Wagon"
Rode him to fortune and to fame!
That's years ago—but Jimmy's skill
is making bully pictures still!

King Vidor

The Big Parade, the Double Door,
The Crowd and La Boheme
So Red the Rose, and several more
Have made King Vidor's fame,
Or putting it more truly, reader,
Their fame was doubtless made by Vidor.

James Whale

James Whale's the director
Who's proved, as we know,
There's no boat like Show Boat
A Whale of a show!

Charles Chaplin

Producer, Director, prop-inspector,
Scenario-writer, camera-sighter,
Low comedian, Heavy Tragedian,
Dancer, singer, extra, star!
He handles all of the jobs there are.
For a Chaplin film, I would beg to bid you all
Kindly to get in your bean or knob,
Is a wholly, solely, individual
Personal Chaplin job!

David Wark Griffith

Here's the old Master whose "Birth of a nation"
Made pulses faster all over creation,
Griffith, presenter of Epics that thrall,
"Close-up" inventor, Sage, Nestor and Mentor
And Dean of them all!

Lew Ayres

Lew Ayres, Republic's new director,
has tasted rue and sampled nectar;
He's been a star, and then a flop,
Then re-ascended to the top;
Directing "Hearts in Bondage," Lew
Rates "Attaboy!" and "Banzai" too.

Richard Boleslawski

We'll have to use a word like "bosky"
To get a rhyme for Boleslawski,
But though his name may puzzle many
"Macbeth" and "Mr. Moneypenny,"
"Vagabond King" and "Men in White"
Are films that give us such delight,
That this jaw-breaking Polish name
Stays in our memory, just the same!

Clarence Brown

Many a picture has "gone to town"
Through smooth direction by Clarence Brown,
Who started by fashioning motor cars
And now accelerates movie stars.
What a galaxy Brown has offered!
Beery, Barrymore, Dressler, Crawford,
Gilbert, Garbo, and Gable too
Taylor, Shearer—are but a few
Of streamlined models who've gone to town
Steered to fortune by Clarence Brown!

William Keighley

A toast to William Keighley
(Who rhymes, it seems, with "steelly")
For films that deal with He-Men
Like "Special Agent," "Ge-Men"
And gentler features, too
For now he seeks "Green Pastures"
Green Pastures that are new.

Sidney Franklin

Don't let gloomy thoughts be ranklin—keep on "Smilin' Through"
with Franklin Like a film that's smart and brainy? See "The Last of
Mrs. Cheyney"
Or "The Guardsman" or "The Barretts"—(Jewels weighing
many carats) If you're such a gem collector, page Sid Franklin as Director.

Gregory La Cava

The work of La Cava
is tasty as guava!
Once newspaper artist, and now a director
Who ranks with the smartest in Hollywood's sector,
His "Private World's" rates all the laurels you toss
And—pin a rose, too, on "She Married Her Boss!"

David O. Selznick

N-I-C-K—that spells "Nick"
And there's a rhyme for Selznick,
Young David, who appealed
With "David Copperfield"
To all the great world's heart
With such consummate art!

Rex Ingram

I'll say Rex Ingram is no slouch—
For he directed Scaramouche!
He surely had a clever touch
When he directed Scaramouche!—
He rates a medal or a brooch
For what he did with Scaramouche!
(Well, go ahead—pronounce it, Bo!
Rex Ingram made it—that I know!)

(reprinted from Cinema Arts, *Vol. 1, No. 1, preview issue, September 1936, pages 37–39)*

Sun at Zenith:
Dedicated to the memory of Irving Thalberg
by Virgil Miller

When old men sleep
After their day is through,
The world walks tiptoe, lest they wake
From pleasant dreams.
But at high noon,
With but the day half through—
Young men lie down to rest awhile
And drift into a dreamless sleep;
Nor wake when working men
Resume their heavy tred. . . .
With so much work to do
Why must we call them dead?

All through the morning hours,
He swiftly, grandly lived;
accomplished much;
Was called, and most deserved, Great;
Yet his forenoon was but a preparation.
How much more great his work had been
With life less incomplete. . . .
Had he but lived
Until the Sunset!

(reprinted from Rob Wagner's Script, *October 3, 1936, page 3)*

Cold Are the Hands of Time
by Preston Sturges

Cold are the hands of time—
   that creep along relentlessly
Destroying slowly
   but without pity
That which yesterday was young.
Alone our memories
   resist this disintegration—
And grow more lovely with the passing years.

(Sturges apparently wrote this in the early thirties; It appears in Rouben Mamoulian's autograph book, dated 1936, and is recited by the "Wienie King" in The Palm Beach Story, *released in 1942)*

Hollywood Rendezvous
(*"Watch the Stars at Play"*)
by Sydney King Russell

Come here to dine
Or come to view
A universe
You never knew.

Here by a chance,
A whim of fate,
A world is yours
To contemplate.

Where you may sit
Alone and brood,
And watch the stars
Devour their food.

And hear the cinema's
Darlings laugh,
Or beg a film star's
Autograph.

Here you may linger
Rapt of eye
To watch the gay
Parade go by.

Here you may loiter
Past eleven
And count the stars
In this strange heaven.

And hear all Hollywood
Discuss
Salaries long since
Fabulous.

While you sit by,
A luckless sinner,
And curse an unappetizing
Dinner.

(reprinted from Rob Wagner's Script, *January 30, 1937, page 5)*

Prayer of a Movie Star
by Grace Evelyn Tobin

O searching camera, please be kind,
And make my tired face unlined;
Don't show my eyes are dim.

Oh, catch my lips so finely carved,
Conceal the fact that I'm half-starved,
Just show that I am slim.

Bring splendor to my fading skin,
Be gentle with that extra chin,
And glorify my smile.

I'll use my strength and brains to act
The brilliant plot somebody's hacked
To suit my so-called style.

Since all the rest depends on you,
If I shine on or if I'm through,
O camera, please be kind.

(reprinted from Rob Wagner's Script, *July 17, 1937, page 5)*

Conference Song of the Studio Bandar-Log
by Peter O'Crotty

Here we go to the Story Room;
Nothing sweeps like a brand-new broom.
Don't you envy our great prestige?
We sweep the world for story needs.
Wouldn't you like if your brains were so
Colossal, gigantic, and slothfully slow?
Now you're angry, but—never mind,
Brother, thy tail hangs down behind!

Here we sit in a paunchy row
Thinking of beautiful things we know;
Dreaming of stuff we mean to shoot
Starring that blonde who is just too cute—
Something noble and grand and good
Won by merely wishing we could.
Now we're going to—never mind,
Brother, thy tail hangs down behind!

All the talk we have ever heard
Uttered by men whose printed word
Made them birds of a different feather;
Still we jabber it all together.
Tremendous! Stupendous! Once again!
Now we are talking just like those men.
Now we're going to—never mind,
Brother, thy tail hangs down behind!
We are the supervisorial kind.

Then join the leaping throngs that scumfish to our previews,
That rocket by, arc-lit on high, attracting critics' reviews.
By the rubbish in our wake, and the noble noise we make,
You can see just why our program calls for new views!

(reprinted from Rob Wagner's Script, *August 28, 1937, page 11)*

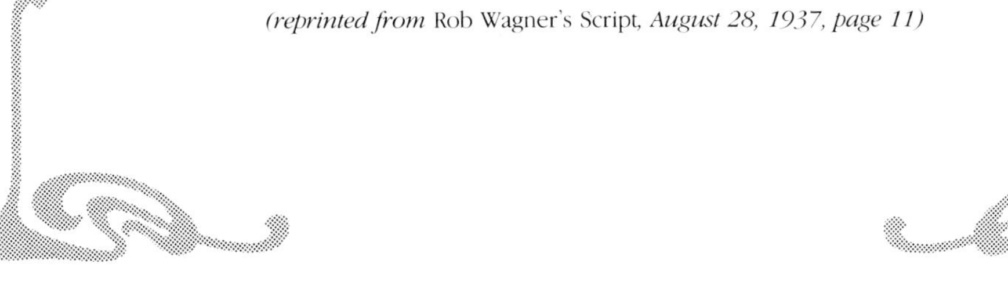

Lo! The Poor Scribe
by M.N.L.

The N.G.O. was a studio of cinematic shame;
Its president, a wily gent, was Minkovitch by name.
With hand on helm, he ruled this realm of Cinemaniacs
And urged them all to "hit the ball" and never to relax.
At promptly eight on any date, Sol Minkovitch was there,
A "frozen phiz" accenting his proprietary air.
And as he'd trot about The Lot in search of fault to find,
His sycophants, like mendicants, would trot along behind.

"Esprit de Corps" was nothing more at dear old N.G.O.
Than constant hope one might promote some other studio—
Each mind intent, each effort bent to temporize and fake
Until the day that they could say "go jump into the lake."
Now Minky's mind had not defined this general unrest
And still pursued by methods crude what it opined was best.
He bawled at all, both great and small, with sanguinary zest
But his assaults on writers' faults were venemously pressed.

He said "Zane Grey is too passé" and "Pooh! for Gertrude Stein,"
"Rupe Hughes is trite" and "Stewart White is worse than Peter Kyne,"
"Anita Loos, like Mother Goose, should stick to nursery rhymes
"But Isidore, my son-in-law, is right up to the times.
"That boy is great," old Sol would state. "Without a word of doubt
"A couple o' leads is all he needs to turn a story out.
"His latest hunch is full o' punch and lots o' Old Magoo—
"With half a chance he'd knock the pants off Dumas and Sardou."

Such words as these would tend to freeze the most prolific brain
That e'er devised or plagiarized for glory or for gain
But Minky thought that he had bought these brains for cash in hand
And why insult brought no result, he couldn't understand.
As any worm will start to squirm if tantalized too much,
His scribes began to form a plan to put old Sol "in Dutch."
The writing staff now ceased to chaff at Minky's son-in-law
And didn't smirk about his work but called on him for more.

Then one fine day Sol heard them say, "We have a great idea—
"This repertoire by Isidore has shown us pretty clear
"That we were wrong to hold out long against such artistry
"And not have seen a mind so keen must win eventually."
The scheme was great—Sol took the bait and said, "It was no bluff;
"That boy is smart and from the start I knew he had the stuff.
"Among the lot, I'm sure we've got a story that'll click,
"So don't let's stall but hit the ball and turn out something, quick."

Well, thus enthused and much amused, the writers "hit the ball."
Each searched his mind and tried to find a tale he could recall
That in the past had been a vast and glorious success
And what they did to Minky's kid it isn't hard to guess.
They made their play in such a way as to convince the lad
That he'd conceived the plot they weaved and satisfied his dad
That even the Academy would notify its Board
They must bestow on N.G.O. the Annual Award.

All thought of cost was promptly tossed aside for this event
And every "hand" at Sol's command was vitally intent
Upon what they were told would pay enormous dividends
And put The Lot into a spot where it could make amends.
"Amends" was right, for it was quite considerable time
Since Minky's stuff was good enough to bring him in a dime.
The dirty slur "No Good Ones" were turned out at N.G.O.
Had hurt his pride and helped decide to make this one a "Go."

Eventually, The Odyssey was "shot" and "in the can."
The pause was brief before the grief of editing began.
The writers saw what was in store if no one "sprung a leak"
And hung around with joy profound, each one with tongue in cheek.
The cutters toiled and Minky moiled from morn till late at night
Without surcease; This Masterpiece just had to come out right
And when at last the word was passed that editing was done,
The Story Staff suppressed a laugh and waited for the fun.

The preview show was scheduled so that everyone was there.
Newspaper men of poison pen were hiding everywhere.
Stars, not a few—Producers too and Agents by the score—
All came to crow that N.G.O. had laid an egg once more
But those who came to flaunt the shame of Minky and his Crew
Remained to cheer and volunteer advice and "ballyhoo."
They tried to guess what this success would bring in gross receipts
And all agreed it would exceed the best of former feats.

This paragon of "bull and con" went over with a bang.
It proved a mint and not a hint of plagiarism's tang
Besmirched its name or dimmed its fame throughout a record run
And dollars piled as Minky smiled at what "his boy" had done.
I think the rest you must have guessed. He canned the Writing Staff
And Isidore, his son-in-law, was "cut in" for half.
Don't tax your mind and try to find a moral for this tale—
It's Breaks, not Brains, and Pull, not Pains, that never seem to fail.

(reprinted from The Screen Guild Magazine, *February 1938, page 18)*

Hollywocky
by Carroll Johnson

Twas garbo and the timmccoy
Did march and baxter in the mix.
All powell were the myrnaloy,
And the disney richarddix.

"Beware the butterworth, my son—
The jaws that bite, the claws that ruin ya.
Beware the landi and irenedunne
The douglasfairbanksjunior!"

And as in hardy thought he stood
The butterworth, with eyes of flame,
Came boland through the ruggles wood
And munied as it came.

One two! One two! and through and through
The gable blade went snicker-snack.
He left it dead and with its head
Went eddiecantoring back.

He took his gable sword in hand;
Long time his karloff foe he sought.
Then rested he 'neath the laurel tree,
And stood awhile in thought.

"And hast thou slain the butterworth?
Come to thy lamour, my boy!
O horton day! O alice faye!"
He crawford in his joy.

Twas garbo and timmccoy
Did march and baxter in the mix
All powell were the myrnaloy
And the disney richarddix.

(reprinted from Rob Wagner's Script, *October 1, 1938, page 8)*

Love Is Where You Find It
by Tad Russell

Lombard's legs
Are quite divine,
But so are my sweetie's
Superfine.

Hedy's form
An ode deserves,
But you should see
My sweetie's curves.

Garbo's kiss
Ambrosia drips,
But you should taste
My baby's lips.

Every close-up
That we share
Makes Love's paradise
More fair.

In short, though
Movie maids galore
Have subtle charms
That men adore,
My pet has all they've got—
And more!

(reprinted from Rob Wagner's Script, *December 10, 1938, page 15)*

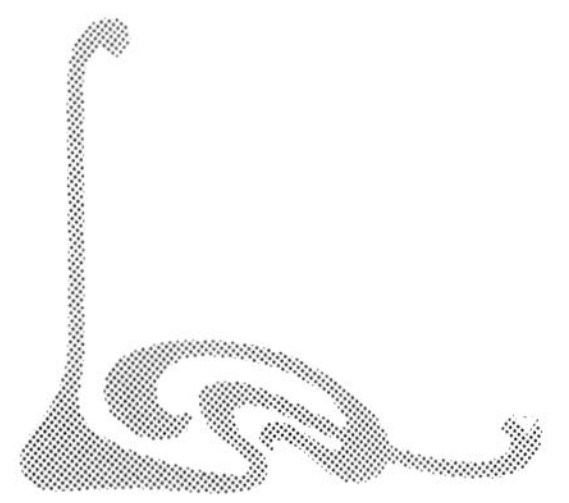

O, Father Time
by Preston Sturges

O, Father Time, lay not thy frost
Upon thy budding flower,
On bitter seas of passion tossed,
Forgive its tiny hour!
And thou, Huguette, waste not thy heart
Upon this juiceless mold,
Ere all thy fragrant youth depart
And leave thee useless . . . old.

(Written by Preston Sturges after the style of Francois Villon; used in the film If I Were King, *released in 1938)*

Clark Gable

Said Clark Gable, picking his nose,
"I get more than the public suppose.
Take the Hollywood way,
It's the women who pay,
And the men simply take off their clothes."

(this anonymous limerick is believed to date from 1939)

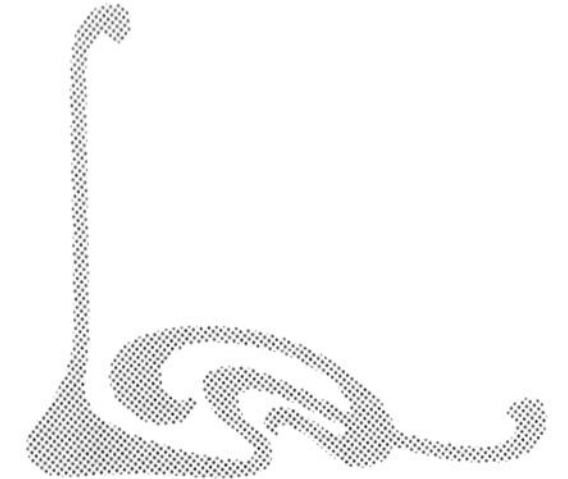

Redskin in Hollywood
by Sydney King Russell

Descendant of a lean and wiry race,
He rides a horse and runs and swims with ease.
A light of other days is on his face,
Echoes of old defeats and victories
Ring in his ears and haunt his dreams at night;
The blood of chieftans courses through his veins
In swift and savage rhythms of delight,
The heritage of children of the plains.

He dons the costume of the early braves—
A white man rules him with a megaphone,
A camera grinds, the flag of freedom waves
And in the sacred name of Movietone
He re-creates the day when, man to man,
The white chief overthrew the Indian.

(reprinted from Rob Wagner's Script, *October 7, 1939, page 23)*

D'Artagnan
(To the Memory of Douglas Fairbanks)*
by Jay Strauss

Those feats of his, he only could perform.
The children would have hooted, did they see
Another, aidless, besting such a storm
Of hulking might and leagued malignity;
Still, we who saw remember, wistfully,
That stalwart figure, Gascon in its pose,
Alone upon a stairway slashing free—
A single sword against a host of foes.
    Oh, then it seemed men might tread down their fears
    Of vanquishment and doom, and undismayed,
    Armed with a just cause, in a splendid rage
    Confound all odds—but even as he played,
    Outside the playhouse, on a sterner stage,
    The tide of woe crept with the graying years.

And those of us whose youth with his youth ceased,
Beheld the world grow old in misery;
The strength of wrong by slavish fear increased,
And the free spirit slain by tyranny;
As perished that heroic chivalry
Sworn to do justice unto men the least,
In that strange battle by the western sea,
When Arthur's realm reeled back into the beast.
    Or so it seemed, till sudden at life's close,
    Just ere the hour of his going forth,
    We saw the old brave faith of man restored,
    Where lone upon the ramparts of the North
    Stood Finland, with the single shining sword
    Of a just cause against a host of foes.

(reprinted from Rob Wagner's Script, *January 6, 1940, page 16)*

*Douglas Fairbanks died on December 12, 1939.

Little Orson Annie*
by Gene Lockhart

Little Orson Annie's come to our town to play,
An' josh the motion pictures up, an' skeer the stars away,
An' shoo the laughtons off the lot, an' build the sets an' sweep,
An' take the film, an' write the talk, an' earn her board-an'-keep;
An' all us other acters, when our pitchur work is done,
We set around the Derby bar an' has the mostest fun,
A-listenin to the *me*-tales 'at Annie spreads about,
An' the Gobble-welles 'at gits you

     Ef you

        Don't

           Watch

             Out!

Onc't there wuz a actor man tried to add a line—
An' when he played a scene in bed and hoped to shine,
His agent heerd him holler, his manager heerd him bawl,
An' when they turn't the kivvers down, he wuzn't there at all!
An' they seeked him in his dressing-room, and told it to the press,
An' seeked him in the Masquers Club, 'an ever'wheres, I guess,
But all they ever found was this, his pants, an' script, an' clout!—
An' the Gobble-welles'll git you

     Ef you

        Don't

           Watch

             Out!

An' one time a ingenue 'ud allus laugh an' grin,
An' giggle at the Orsonwoof, and at his discipline;
An' onc't when they wuz in a scene, an' "company" wuz there,
She mocked him, an' she shocked him, an' said she didn't care!
An' thist as she kicked up her heels an' turn't to run an' hide,
They wuz a great big Brown Beard a-stridin' by her side,
An' it *snatched* her from the pitchur 'fore she knowed what she's about!
An' the Gobble-welles'll git you

  Ef you

   Don't

    Watch

     Out!

An' little Orson Annie says, when the talk is blue,
An' the camera splutters, an' the sound goes whoo!
An' you hear the scrip' girl quake, an' the crew looks gray,
An' the casting-office man has faint-ed away—
You better mind yer cues an' yer director fond an' dear,
An' churish him 'at hired you, an' 'bedient appear,
An' he'p the pore old Fuddledy Beard 'at rushes all about,
Er the Gobble-welles'll git *you*

  Ef you

   Don't

    Watch

     Out!

(reprinted from Rob Wagner's Script, *January 27, 1940, page 4)*

Citizen Kane, directed by Orson Welles, was released in 1941; Gene Lockhart was a popular character actor on stage and screen.

Hollywood Parade
by Sydney King Russell

Old Actor
In Hollywood they know him as The Ghost—
He was an actor long ago, whose fame
Preceded him from eager coast to coast,
Who won his public's worshipful acclaim.
Now no one turns at mention of his name;
His generation passes . . . and he goes
Obscurely, laboring to play the game,
An outcast from the only world he knows.

When movie mobs convene, you may depend,
None recognizes in that cavalcade
The white-haired extra, second from the end
Who seldom thinks to mention that he played
With Kean and Sothern once upon a time
And shared a scene with Mansfield in his prime.

Blonde
Behind the counter in a a Ten Cent Store
She waits on customers from nine to five
And thinks in silence of the days before
She reached the Melting Pot, where thousands strive
To win a glowing goal that few attain.
"Crawford and Shearer made it—why not I?
What have they got that I—?" Her puzzled brain
Gropes for the answer that eludes her, *Why?*

To casting-offices she sends with care
Her photographs in calculated poses
Like those in movie magazines. Aware
that life at best is not a bed of roses,
She sells cosmetics, sealing wax, and soap
And learns to live on hamburgers and hope.

Hollywood Mother
She harbors the maternal zeal of one
Who knows her child, the apple of her eye,
Deserves a place, like Shirley, in the sun,
A destiny that no one would deny—
When she has bleached the little darling's hair
She trains it into tight and tempting curls,
And teaches her the pout and baby stare
That spell the lure of countless glamor girls.

Such artistry as Mary Ann discloses
Would send her public into ecstasies,
She argues, while her agent nods and dozes,
But though producers beg her on their knees,
She will not sell her daughter—not for less
Than stardom's wage, the symbol of success.

Press Agent
With fertile brain he cleverly invents
Colorful pasts for picture stars who need
A background. With the cunning of pretense
He fashions legends for a world to read.
Because of him most readers are aware
That Rose Malone sprang from a royal line
Of princesses—that handsome Donald Dare
Once led the choir at the age of nine.

Such pasts as otherwise would need concealing
He touches up a bit with quiet tact,
And leaves his readers with the pleasant feeling
That all his narratives are based on fact,
Which is a gift, when duly cultivated,
Not to be lightly underestimated.

(reprinted from Rob Wagner's Script, *February 3, 1940, page 3)*

For a Certain Cowboy Gone West
(Will Rogers)
by Irene Wilde

When time's long tether broke and set you free
On some horizonless, far Western range,
Finding your way, you rode familiarly
Along the starry trails that were not strange,
Surveyed the horns of Taurus unabashed;
And when the reckless dark let down the bars,
Lean thigh upon your mustang's flank you dashed
Against the peril of stampeding stars.
You galloped through the thundering herd of night
Humming a stave of some old prairie tune,
And with a gesture, versatile and light,
You hurled your lariat around the moon.

(reprinted from Rob Wagner's Script, *February 24, 1940, page 3)*

The Ballad of Gower's Gulch
by Gene Lockhart

Now this is the ballad of Gower's Gulch,
Whar the sun drops down in the west,
Whar the cowboys drop in at the Ex-Lax Saloon
An' the cokes drop down on their vest.

A rough but a right honest bunch they were,
Them cowboys an' rustlers, an' all,
A-wranglin' their lunch, a chewin' the fur,
An' a-waitin' a studio call.

Among all them cowboys around Gower's Gulch,
Wuz two who wuz mighty good friends,
We'll jes' call 'em Bill an' Ole Lew fer the now;
You'll see how my story ends.

Now Bill, he waz one of the surest shots,
The way he could shoot wuz a shame,
An' he allus collected the biggest pots
When he shot in the marble game.

An Lew, he wuz spry with the cards, d'y'see,
His good luck he allus filled,
Fer the cards in his pockets were marked, d'y'see,
Afra an' screen acters guild.

I'll give ye the facts, jes' how it occurred,
The fight, and the shootin' spree;
I'll give it ye straight, I'll give word fer word,
An' you'll know as much as me.

Well, Lew, he gets mad at ole Bill one day—
Or Bill, he gets mad at Lew;
It don't matter much whose billing comes first,
The fightin' features the two.

So Lew—or Bill—he starts in to swear
At the other fer things he has done,
An' Bill—or Lew—he sez, "now take care
Afore any trouble's begun";

Well, Lew—or Bill—had been lappin' up cokes,
So he whips out a gun, or a knife,
An' Bill—or Lew—the t'other he soaks
An' one of 'em runs fer his life.

Well, whut happened next wuz whut happened to me.
I quit that fight pronto, that's all;
For they hollered to me from the Ex-Lax Saloon
An' give me a studio call!

(reprinted from Rob Wagner's Script, *March 9, 1940, page 18)*

Leaven
by Inez Firenza

*The kingdom of heaven is like unto leaven, which a woman took,
and hid in three measures of meal, till the whole was leavened.*
—Matthew 13:33

I saw *The Grapes of Wrath*—
I saw Ma Joad.
Did you see Ma Joad?
I want to give Ma Joad a satin comforter
And costly perfume and a foolish hat.
Have you a satin comforter and costly perfume
And a foolish hat?

I saw *The Grapes of Wrath*—
I saw Tom Joad.
Did you see Tom Joad?
I want to give Tom Joad a shining motor car
And vintage champagne and a silk cravat.
Have you a shining motor car and vintage champagne
And a silk cravat?

(reprinted from Rob Wagner's Script, *June 22, 1940, page 29)*

Bergen's Boy*
by Gene Lockhart

Blessings on thee, little man,
Bergen's boy with pixy pan;
With thy laughing lacquered face,
And thy eye-glass glued in place;
With thy bergintoned harpoons,
And thy slyly aimed slampoons;
With thy ad-libs, glibber still,
Ribbing others on the bill,
To our hearts thou givest joy,
Saplinguistic Bergen's boy!

Cap-and-bells of renaissance
Are thy true inheritance;
But that motley tattered cap
Now's a shiny opera hat;
And thy ancient jester's cape
Is a coat of tailored shape;
And thy laughter-making throne
Is a chromium microphone;
While the bells that herald thee
Are three bongs from N.B.C.

Perched upon the social ladder
With thy verbal stick-and-bladder,
Spoofing all the stiff and proud
With a noise both long and loud,
Uttering in thy whimsy way
All the things we'd like to say,
Thou art now the gratifier
Of a long suppressed desire;
Worth in gold thy total weight,
(Cf. current Crosley rate).

Real thou art: that grown-up man
Merely aids thy Puckish plan;
He may think he pulls a string:
I deny he does a thing!
For I've seen thee breathe and wink,
Slowly pause, and slyly think.
O! what fools we mortals be!
Not to live and laugh like thee;
Chase's pride and Sanborn's joy,
Blessings on thee, Bergen's boy.

(reprinted from Rob Wagner's Script, *February 22, 1941, page 17)*

*A reference to Edgar Bergen's dummy, Charlie McCarthy, who, with Bergen, entertained millions on screen and on radio in the Chase and Sanborn Show.

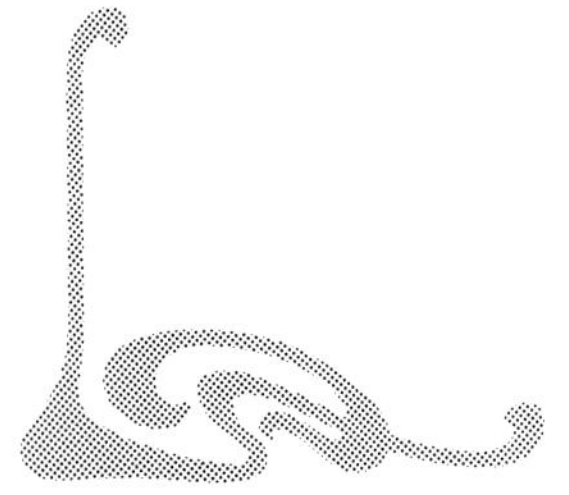

Hollywood Agent
by Sydney King Russell

He used to peddle books from door to door
And gadgets for the housewives to employ,
He sold subscriptions, tackled any chore
As long as there were prospects to annoy.
But now he deals in other merchandise,
Since talent has its price in Hollywood—
Beauty and youth he shrewdly sells and buys
And gets his price, as a wise salesman should.

He used to deal in neckties, socks and collars,
Economize, and count his meagre fees,
But now he has some eighty thousand dollars
Salted away in sound securities,
For now he peddles flesh, forever bent
Upon his premium of ten per cent.

(reprinted from Rob Wagner's Script, *January 31, 1942, page 8)*

Joan Bennett

Since donning a uniform, Joe
Quit the floozies that he used to know.
Says he, "Joan Bennett'll
Tickle my genital
Every night at the old U.S.O."

(this anonymous limerick is believed to date from 1944)

Errol Flynn

It's a helluva fix that we're in
When the geographical spread of the urge to sin
Causes juvenile delinquency
With increasing frequency
By the Army, the Navy, and Errol Flynn.

(this anonymous limerick is believed to date from 1947)

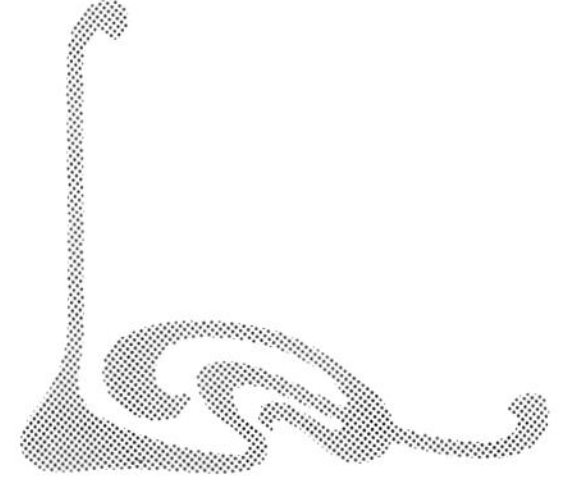

A Review of *Charley's Aunt**
by C.A. Lejeune

Can you think of any
Reason why Jack Benny
Should play Charley's Aunt?
I can't.

(reprinted from Chestnuts in Her Lap *by C.A. Lejeune, London: Phoenix House, 1947)*

**Charley's Aunt* was released by 20th Century-Fox in 1941; it starred Jack Benny, Kay Francis and Anne Baxter, and was directed by Archie Mayo.

A Review of *Saigon**
by C.A. Lejeune

Another bygone
Theme like Saigon,
And I've had
Alan Ladd.

(reprinted from Chestnuts in Her Lap *by C.A. Lejeune, London: Phoenix House, 1947)*

**Saigon* was released by Paramount in 1948; it starred Alan Ladd, Veronica Lake and Douglas Dick, and was directed by Leslie Fenton.

A Review of *Humoresque**
by C.A. Lejeune

In this long rapture of pretence
There is one moment of good sense,
When Crawford (J), a female souse,
Displays a modicum of *nous*.

On hearing Wagner's *Liebestod*
Performed the way it wasn't wrote,
She proves her musical devotion
By walking straight into the ocean.

(reprinted from Chestnuts in Her Lap *by C.A. Lejeune, London: Phoenix House, 1947)*

**Humoresque* was released by Warner Bros. in 1946; it starred Joan Crawford and John Garfield, and was directed by Jean Negulesco.

To Joan Crawford
by Robert E. Henson

For two hours life will have some point, while rain
Falls on Main Street and the smell of hot
Popcorn hangs beneath the lights. Now plain
Girls sleep and dream, from common folks whose lot
Has nothing of this glittering tale—the lack
But emphasized and given form anew:
The quilts that smell of bacon grease; the back
Steps broken; dime store lipstick; and so few
Who understand the "I am different . . ." Yet *she*
Was once a walker in this dream, a mouse,
A cinderella . . . Not the presidency
Alone is wrought by firelight in the loghouse.

Outside the beer joint, then, this baffled view
Of Ruby wearing, borrowed, something new.

(reprinted from Script, *September 1948, page 19)*

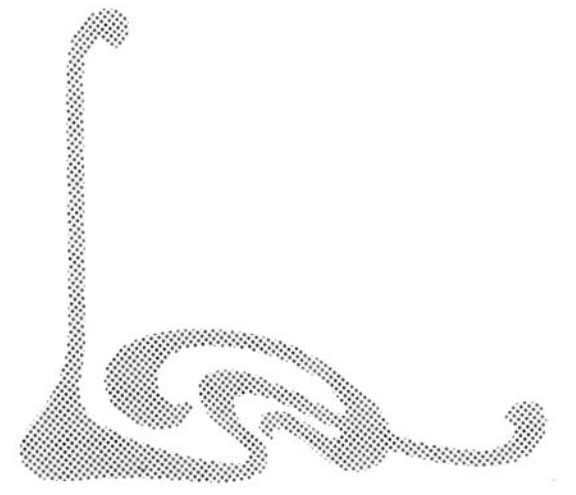

To Mr. Mack Sennett, on His Animated Pictures
by Morris Bishop

SENNETT! Regard, I pray, our cinema—
   Its endless reels of rancid agonies,
The drear dilemmas of its formula.
   There is no laughter in Los Angeles.

CHAPLIN, arouse! Up, up, my HAROLD LLOYD!
   Ah, where is CONKLIN? MABEL NORMAND, where?
Only the coils of Technicolored FREUD
   Discharge their nonsense on the shuddering air.

Betimes a notice strikes the casual eye:
   "You'll scream, you'll yell, you'll whoop at A or B!
You'll foam and froth and faint at X and Y!"
   Let others titter. They amuse not me.

Ah, no. I'll bid old memories arise,
   Let the dead pan of LANGDON soothe my soul,
Watch TURPIN roll his independent eyes,
   And the flung custard seek its human goal.

(reprinted from The New Yorker, *January 22, 1949, page 30)*

Nobody Dies Like Humphrey Bogart
by Norman Rosten

Casual at the wheel, blinding rainstorm,
The usual blonde doll alongside—only
This time our man knows she's talked,
The double-c, and by his cold eyes
We can tell it's the end of the line for her.

It's all in the corner of his mouth:
Baby if we're gonna go we'll both go
My way, and his foot deep on the gas
With the needle (close-up) leaping to eighty.
She's shaky but ready to call his bluff.

Rain and the wipers clearing the glass
And dead ahead the good old roadblock.
Quick shot moll—the scream forming.
Quick shot Bogey—that endearing look
Which was his alone, face and soul.

Any way we go, baby, one or the other,
You'll look a lot prettier than me
When we're laid out in the last scene,
You in pink or blue with the angels,
Me with the same scar I was born in.

(first published in 1955)

Horror Movie
by Howard Moss

Dr. Unlikely, we love you so,
You who made the double-headed rabbits grow
From a single hare. Mutation's friend,
Who could have prophecied the end
When the Spider Woman deftly snared the fly
And the monsters strangled in a monstrous kiss
And somebody hissed, "You'll hang for this!"?

Dear Dracula, sleeping on your native soil,
(Any other kind makes him spoil),
How we clapped when you broke the French door down
And surprised the bride in the overwrought bed.
Perfectly dressed for lunar research,
Your evening cape added much,
Though the bride, inexplicably dressed in furs,
Was a study in jaded jugulars.

Poor tortured Leopard Man, you changed your spots
In the debauched village of the Pin-Head Tots;
How we wrung our hands, how we wept
When the eighteenth murder proved inept,
And, caught in the Phosphorus Cave of Sea,
Dangling the last of synthetic flesh,
You said, "There's something wrong with me."

The Wolf Man knew when he prowled at dawn
Beginnings spin a web where endings spawn.
The bat who lived on shaving cream,
A household pet of Dr. Dream,
Unfortunately, maddened by the bedlam,
Turned on the Doc, bit the hand that fed him.

And you, Dr. X, who killed by moonlight,
We loved your scream in the laboratory
When the panel slid and the night was starry
And you threw the inventor in the crocodile pit
(An obscure point: Did he deserve it?)
And you took the gold to Transylvania
Where no one guessed how insane you were.

We thank you for the moral and the mood,
Dear Dr. Cliche, Nurse Platitude.
When we meet again by the Overturned Grave,
Near the Sunken City of the Twisted Mind,
(In The Son of the Son of Frankenstein),
Make the blood flow, make the motive muddy:
There's a little death in every body.

(first published 1957)

Movie House
by John Updike

View it, by day, from the back,
from the parking lot in the rear,
for from this angle only
The beautiful brick blackness can be grasped.
Monumentality
wears one face in all ages.

No windows intrude real light
into this temple of shades,
and the size of it,
the size of the great rear wall measures
the breadth of the dreams we have had here.
It dwarfs the village bank,
outlooms the town hall,
and even in its decline
makes the bright-ceilinged supermarket seem mean.

Stark closet of stealthy rapture,
vast introspective camera
wherein our most daring self-projections
were given familiar names:
stand, stand by your macadam lake
and tell the aeons of our extinction
that we too could house our gods,
could secrete a pyramid
to sight the stars by.

(reprinted from Telephone Poles and Other Poems *by John Updike, New York: Alfred A. Knopf, 1963)*

Reel One
by Adrien Stoutenburg

It was all technicolor
from bullets to nurses.
The guns gleamed like cars
and blood was as red
as the paint on dancers.
The screen shook with fire
and my bones whistled.
It was like life but better.

I held my girl's hand,
in the deepest parts,
and we walked home, after,
with the snow falling,
but there wasn't much blue
in the drifts or corners:
just white and more white
and the sound track so dead
you could almost imagine
the trees were talking

(reprinted from Heroes, Advise Us *by Adrien Stoutenburg, New York: Charles Scribner's Sons, 1964)*

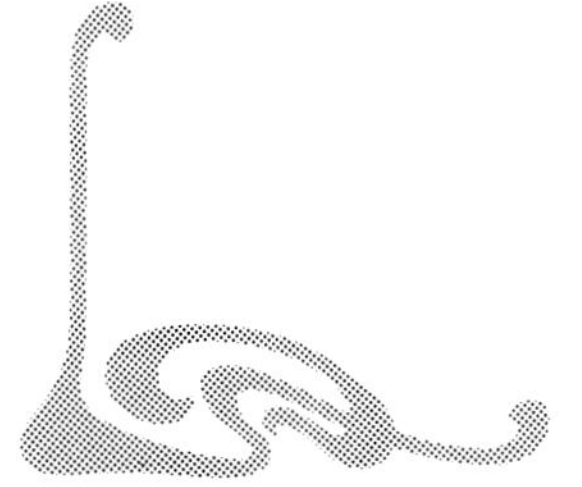

The Day I Stopped Dreaming about Barbara Steele*
by R.H.W. Dillard

The drizzle shifted,
A bird drowsy with rain
Yawned into song,
The foghorn ran down.

Below the castle walls
Her head grisly with masks
The long slices of her sides
And the heavy dog's howl
(I hear the clamor of horses
    And the long rope to which I am attached
    Buckles beneath me)
The knotted arm
And the long sinew
That lays itself along
The long curve of her side.

Blond, her legs curved
To the horse's flank,
Making the sun dance
To the blue of her eyes.

(Is the last dream before waking
More flesh than real,
More real than the dark before?)

The horse dances
And she is as purely naked
As the pine-needled dawn
And the dogs run lazy and smooth
In the tall grass.

The bronze door,
Stone,
A muffled cry,
The iron maiden,
And the sun
Crazy with its own size
In the moving lake
Where her horse lowers its head to drink
And she sleeps on his arching spine.

(reprinted from The Day I Stopped Dreaming about Barbara Steele *by R.H.W. Dillard, Chapel Hill, N.C.: The University of North Carolina Press, 1966)*

*Born in the United Kingdom in 1938, Barbara Steele is best known for the horror films in which she has appeared, including *The Pit and the Pendulum* (1961), *Revenge of the Blood Beast* (1966) and *Curse of the Crimson Altar* (1968).

Jack the Ripper*
by Charles Higham

I

He put his hands down, down
Into the black waters
Of the River Thames

Crying, where, where
Else is there peace, for these
Restless probing fingers

Which once quietly
Moved on the slack strings
Or tautly gripped

The knife-haft, gag,
And other modes of death?
Only in the black

Cold sweeping flow
Like sleep lapping
The closed clay—

Muffling all sounds,
Stiffling the brain's cry
That no one hears

Stilling the voices
Of the prostitutes
On the muddy corners.

Oh let there be stillness!
Let the whistles quiet!
Let him into the dark!

II

Once there was a girl with eyes so full of pain
That even the closed lids could not conceal it.
She stood on a wind-beaten bank and held him, crying
Assuage it, assuage it, cut it out of me.
And he tried, in the chilling dusk and the brown fog
Of the valley, to still that pain
As she fell in his arms, she thanked him quietly.

Oh Jack, Jack, she cries now, Jack they are calling you,
My darling in the London rain, my own sad darling
With your instruments of healing, your dark cloak
And face calm as the moon under the tall black hat.
Your smile was never sweeter than when you gave me death.
And now it is only a transference
From pain to pain and now it can never end
And I am to be joined by the others you have killed.

III

One night he slipped away
Out of the rotting pages
Of life's insane book,

No one saw him again,
Though many confessed
On gallows and in beds of death.

The fact is, he's always here,
Moving among us silently,
Ready to strike for peace;

To cleanse the dark thing
Growing inside us,
To ease us of sorrowing,

Like a raven in the dusk
Standing with huge dark eyes
Waiting, always waiting,

His love like a reaching hand
Full of glittering steel
To seek out the white cancer—

Until the very end,
Of each and every city
Jack stands and smiles with a tremendous pity.

(reprinted from Noonday Country *by Charles Higham, Sydney, Australia: Angus and Robertson, 1966)*

*This poem was written after a screening of *The Lodger* (1926), directed by Alfred Hitchcock, and starring Ivor Novello.

Vampire*
by Charles Higham

At midnight, wind
Stripping my skin, I turn
Tight as a screw
To see across fields the moon
Stalking, and firs stand
Like spinsters stiff against life.

I let my cloak fall.
I feel the delicate threads
Of spiders
With the stiff lightness of feathers
Drag down my flesh,
Winding a silken shroud, a death-cocoon.

Pared like fruit
Blackened in fall, I wait love's knife.
She comes, bearing it,
That princess, slits my heart
And I can go
Released from bones, skin, hair,

Light as a parasol
Turned inside out by the wind.
Spines, webs, taut wings,
Eyes like blue coals, tong claws.
And spin a spiral
Of black joy up the tower

To pounce on her,
That frail girl in her bed of glass,
And with my fang
Of purest ivory, inspect her throat.
She does not dread
Me now, but rises, rises,

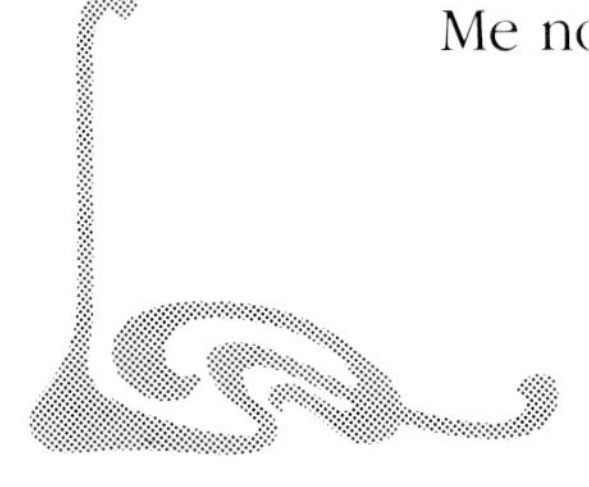

Holding my furred form
To her, feeling the blood that courses
    To my own throat, with
An exultant calm. Her loins are not
    Touched, yet she still
May be called a bride. Of darkness.

    O the wind! The wind!
It calls me from her, I fly like a holly
    Leaf across fields
To black trees I know well, a lake of ice
    I course, seeing,
No image, for I cannot reflect,

    To the drab Carpathians
And crowded villages, huddled like beasts,
    Where under roofs
Of smoking aspen, they wait by the chimneys,
    Those women who know
I will come to them, a lover.

    I can give them life,
And succor, like a furred paw close their mouths
    And still their cravings.
Through me, they breathe
    Dark waters, through me
They course with the sap of lichens.

    Come with me, out
Of that flesh which binds you, blood
    Which repeats in
Limbs like a knell, reminding,
    Reminding you
Of your mortality, of pain

    Instead, soar
With me to the sky's icy surf, or plunge
    Down wheat fields that
Never end, stricken with fire,
    Black corridors
Leading to an ashen moon.

I can end desire!
In my arms all things are still!
  Let your love course
Down my wings and walk
  Streaming with
The banners of a thousand armies!

  And as dawn breaks
Avoiding that lean monk with his stake
  And book of prayers
I will leave you, out in the wood,
  Asleep, asleep,
On the mossed roots of the upas-tree
  Without a dream.

(reprinted from The Hudson Review, *Vol. XX, No. 4, Winter 1967–1968, pages 571–573)*

*Intended as a tribute to all movies of the vampire genre.

Sternberg: In Memoriam*
by Charles Silver

Two fat men await the new arrival at the gates of Hell.
Claudius bears him no love,
but, despite the boss-lady's rules,
the Reichskultursenator has shed a promised tear
for the Jewish boy from Brooklyn—
the greatest Galicianer of them all.

This week Galatea will be 67, so much older than Lola-Lola, Lily, and those other
sublime figments of his imagination.
This week we are all so much older.

"When a director dies, he becomes a photographer."
No, John! When a director dies, he becomes a corpse.
That Jo has been among the dead for 15 years is partly your fault.
It was a long journey from Morroco to Macao,
but an even longer one after that: standing still, till now.

Professor Unrat has gone back to his classroom for the last time;
Don Pasqual will not recover from this wound;
Amy Jolly has died of thirst in the desert.
At last, the flesh has been buried, and only the celluloid still breathes.

Except when the museum curators permit it,
the romantics will have to hunt for their salvation somewhere else,
for there will be no more von in the Chinese laundry.

(reprinted from The Village Voice, *January 8, 1970, page 51)*

*Josef von Sternberg (1894–1969) began his directorial career with *The Salvation Hunters* in 1925; among his other films are *The Blue Angel* (1930), *Morocco* (1930), *The Scarlet Empress* (1934), and *Macao* (1952). He published his autobiography, *Fun in a Chinese Laundry*, in 1965.

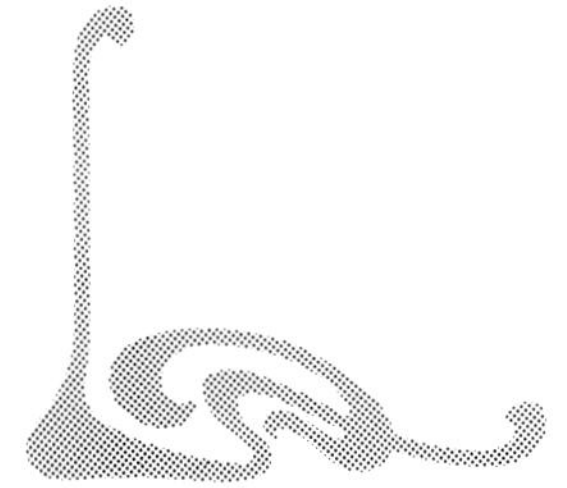

The Physical Imperfections of Old Films
by Paul Ramsey

We enter the darkened hall.
We look upon the dead
Who were sad even then.
The film is running. See,
He is kissing her. She
lifts a hand to his face
As their faces touch. See,
Little lights from nowhere
Interpose their kiss. Let
It be so, let light shine.
Let it be brown, odd light.
Let us not demand it.
For the faces which kiss
Are dead now, and lack means
Of bargaining. So we,
As we take our places,
Also lack means. Let us
Be ready for the light.
It is weakness which shines,
The celluloid's weakness,
But it is shining. It,
Unproposed, beautiful,
Is shining. It shines now.

(copyright 1972)

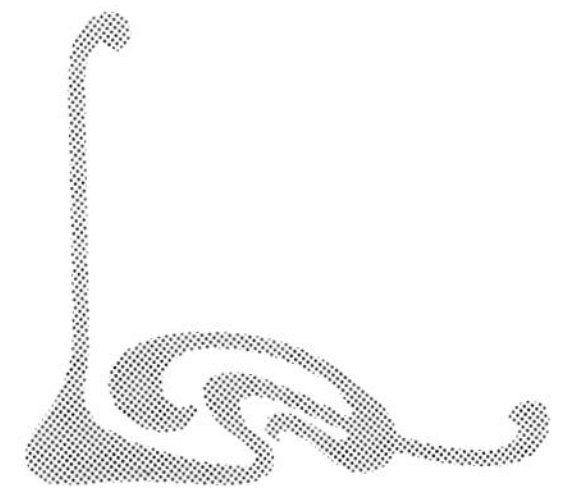

Marilyn Monroe

Marilyn Monroe
by Paul Ramsey

She had a way with comedy and men.
She had a way with words. She loved to act.
Her shyness, beauty shall not come again,
And many of us are saddened by that fact.

(copyright 1972)

Dick Powell
by Ronald Koertge

I saw him in Hollywood yesterday and I asked
him why he even considered acting in those little
T.V. dramas where he was cast as a farmer and
Some tow-headed little bastard who wanted to grow
up to be a potato called him Pa and he was too
old to ever get the creamy ingenue.

And whatever happened to the Dick Powell everybody
loved in "Gold Diggers of 1933" where Ruby Keeler
and Joan Blondell never wore bras but he was too
cool to fall for that because all he wanted to
do was tickle those ivories.

He didn't answer, of course, just stared
until I turned to leave. Then he came for me.

The police separated us eventually and I apologized
for being rude and he mumbled something about
unusual pressures.

But that was days ago and I should have forgotten
all about it but at night and sometimes in the
afternoons and even as I write this I can still
feel those cold, yellow teeth in my bones.

(first published 1973)

Natani Nez: Print the Legend*
by Charles Silver

Ride Tall Soldier, and America rides with you.
   Out of the past—into forever.
From Thoreau's Maine woods came Jack the Mick
   to ride with Cheyenne Harry,
   two noble sons of the prairie,
Phantom riders out of the past—into
   forever.

Round the bend came Dr. Will and Victor,
   the gentle giant,
The Ringo Kid, Brittles and Thornton and Yorke
   all the spawn of the myth they call Duke,
Phantom riders out of the past—into
   forever.

Before Donovan's Reef there was Doniphon's
   wreath, a prairie cactus rose,
A proper laurel on balance for the plain
   pine box of the quiet man,
The legend who shot Liberty Valance.

They returned his boots as they laid him
   to rest in Shinbone—once upon a time in the West.
Put your boots on John; all the others
   have gone.
And you've come to the end of your quest.
Ride Tall Soldier, and America rides with you.
Out of the past—into forever.

(reprinted from Film Comment, *January–February 1974, page 55)*

*A tribute to director John Ford.

Buster Keaton & The Cops
by George Keithley

Stone Face is the likeness of all lovers.
Under a flower cart he keeps his seat,
hiding his hopes from the crowd
until some clown discovers
his hat in the cop-cluttered street.

The officers fall on their knees
in the flowers and find his hiding-place.
He remains undismayed.
He rubs his cuffs and dusts his collar.
The cops crawl up and greet him face to face.

He throws his roses in their eyes.
In retreat he duels for his life,
with daffodils he clouts their clubs.
He creeps from his cart, he tries
to lose them in the lilies which he spills.

When he impeccably plucks his hat
and races through the swirling street,
his shirt-tail hangs unfurled
and waves goodbye to his heart
and goodbye to the fragrant world.

(reprinted from Song in a Strange Land *by George Keithley, New York: George Braziller, 1974)*

On Viewing *Love Crazy**
by Stuart M. Kaminsky

In darkness with a lifeless dream
and the clatter of an old projector,
I raise my arm to break the dusty beam
and cast a shadow at the grinning vector
of William Powell who by me bereft
of voice growls off with a witty pun.
Then his image too is cancelled so I am left
with the clack of film in its certain run
from reel to reel. Then a flick and that
too I take away. Nothing to hear
in total basement darkness but my purring cat
quivering in the silence, sensing human fear.
I breathe. In time and with uncertain finger
return the ghost of Powell who will linger
with me on the wall to forestall confusion
and let me linger in the myth of illusion.

(reprinted from The Journal of Popular Film, *Vol. IV, No. 3, 1975, page 235)*

Love Crazy was released by M-G-M in 1941; it starred William Powell and Myrna Loy, and was directed by Jack Conway.

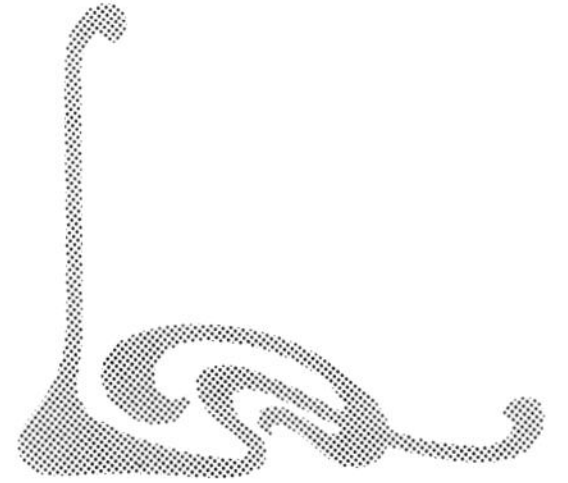

Ozzie Nelson Dead of Cancer
by Ronald Koertge

"The Adventures of Ozzie and Harriet" were bland
as sleep: Ozzie needed a new tie, Ozzie had eaten
too much down at the malt shop, Harriet wanted
a light bulb from upstairs, David and Ricky argued
over a ball, their voices soft as sheets.

Theirs was a home without a toilet, without
bills, without tears. There no one masturbated
or was afraid of God, there no one yelled
or crushed things. They ate and slept, rising
in perfect order to greet that day's dilemma,
not larger than a dot.

What a loss, Mr. Nelson, Ozzie of Ozzies, perfect
husband and father.

This poem of admiration, black upon white like alien
hands in truce, comes too late as it did
for my own father, as different from you
as lamb's wool is from flesh.

But now,
I miss you both.

(first published 1975)

Buster Keaton in *The Navigator* (1924)

The Aristocrat
by John Bricuth*

Buster with his pork-pie hat above
That stone face, no fist, cop's foot, not curled
Lip, no eyes like angry marbles could
Dislodge or nudge the stiff agreement of
That fragile pair, possessed of authority because,
Silent within, at once self-amusing
And self-amused, he kept the personal style
That keeps through common nonsense an iron grace.

In vaudeville with a knockabout act he bent
Body to will, objects into props,
Renewing the aristocratic tradition of
Anything for the laugh. We are a mob in darkness,
Roaring our dangerous approval at the one
Who fights us, grave of face, to keep his hat.

(reprinted from The Heisenberg Variations *by John Bricuth, Athens: University of Georgia Press, 1975)*

*pseudonym of John T. Irwin.

Laurel and Hardy

Laurel and Hardy
For Larry and Faith
by John Bricuth*

I

wide tie, wing collars, vest, and derby hats—
                              "don't
you kick *me* in the shin"—that spiff
boiled front of salad days—"you . . .
keep your distance"—the thin and the fat
ruined gentleman aiming a delirious
Ford with a broken knee, huffing
an upright piano
ten flights up,
fishing off a dock—"tell me,
why can't *we* ever get ahead"—
on the bum
              in the soup
(fish peddlers, Foreign Legionnaires),
battling against the odds to keep odd jobs,
say "Easy Come, Easy Go,"
slipping a bull fiddle to a Pullman berth,
hey, I was in the war, Mac—yeah, ya big "Beau Hunks,"
the race for their hats in the street's high wind,
Politest before a fight—
                              what is it fulfills expectation?—
hearing the cuckoo march, we
anticipate
              the primness in Ollie's Danish pastry fingers
testing the tip of a punched nose,
the miffed wince when cops call him, "Fatty," say
   "move along, Fatty,"
the fluttered tie and tiny smile, the helpless
"why don't you do something to *help* me?" or
"here's another fine mess . . . ,"

know
Stanley's shovel-footed gait, half-moon grin,
in danger of falling
asleep, telling the truth—"don't you *dare*
touch that ladder"—leaning
head on hand
to miss completely

II

but, in fact,
Laurel was the brains of the team,
cold, aloof, English,
a fierce woman-chaser, married eight times,
demanding always twice Hardy's salary,
while Babe,
who'd dance like a bear
for biscuits and honey,
thought (faint drawl and courtly manners)
his real life started at forty-five
                              when,
                                    marrying,
he found untrue what he had believed for years—
no woman could love a fat, comic man

III

what is real?
Arthur Stanley Jefferson
                      and Norvell Hardy?
these two and their two roles make four
and those four one where
playing his opposite each
defeats the other
                  close your eyes—
there is the light-involving frame full
of a motion that is like music, discontinuous

yet finding its continuity in us, frame
supplanting, unmaking frame as note
displaces note
in movements of ablative grace
                                        we
are the dark interpreters of the lighted square,
taught to see two dimensions as three, taught
to feel depth as time and time as depth,
the music plays itself out in us
O
melodic and relentless demolition—
ties clipped, pants ripped—who falls
through the chimney to the basement
bringing the house down with him yelling
"wohoohohoo Oh!" and sits
till the last brick drops "pock"
on his head
                to be
what it is about,
                    to be used up
these lives are the self-dissolving counterpoint
the music plays itself out in us

IV

that Ollie spent his last three years in a wheelchair,
paralyzed, unable to speak, the aristocratic
acrobat's lightness gone, light
dying on a coarsened face,
that Stanley and his last wife tried to live
in a beachfront apartment (dingy
with the bright sunlight of Santa Monica)
on a monthly government check
proves only
true lives are lived
                    moment to moment
by those

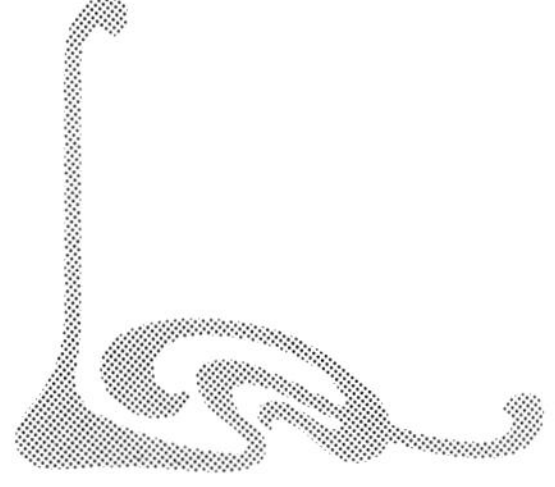

helpless to settle accounts
or save
        money,
                themselves, since these
end
    with nothing,
                or very little,
beyond the perfected gesture
                        and the stance
what is true? suppose
someone says, what is true?
say,
    the truth is time
devours his sons,
and say,
each moment slays the one before,
its father,
and in turn, is slain.

(reprinted from The Heisenberg Variations *by John Bricuth, Athens: University of Georgia Press, 1975)*

*pseudonym of John T. Irwin

In Memory of James Wong Howe*
by Charles Higham

A cool wind
leaves bright water
and finds another place

A bird too lovely
for the dark world
flies to a white branch

There can be no mourning
for those who leave themselves
imprinted on life's
book.

(reprinted from American Cinematographer, *October 1976, page 1159)*

*James Wong Howe (1899–1976) was a major American cinematographer whose films include *The Thin Man* (1934), *Yankee Doodle Dandy* (1942), *Hud* (1963), and *Funny Lady* (1975).

To Humphrey Bogart*
by James Cagney

In this silly town of ours,
One sees odd primps and poses;
But movie stars in fancy cars,
Shouldn't pick their famous noses

(reprinted from Cagney by Cagney, *Garden City, New York: Doubleday, 1976)*

*Written after seeing Humphrey Bogart stopped at a traffic light on Coldwater Canyon in Beverly Hills; he was sitting in a brand new Porsche and picking his nose.

Clark Gable
by James Cagney

The King, long bled, is newly dead.
Uneasily wore his crown, 'tis said;
Quite naturally, since it was made of lead;
On those who gathered about his throne,
Y-clept Mayer, Mannix, Katz, and Cohn
He spat contempt in generous doses,
But whatever he gave, they made their own.

Unhappy man, he chose seclusion,
To the unremitting crass intrusion
Of John and Jane whose names meant dough
To Louie, Eddie, Sam, and Joe.

(reprinted from Cagney by Cagney, *Garden City, New York: Doubleday, 1976)*

So Red the Rose, However You Spell It
by Ogden Nash

Margaret Sullavan, Lovely Meg,
Tell me the reason, pray,
That you spell your name, O bewitching dame,
Sullavan with an a.
Do the Murphys fashion their tag with e,
Or the Finnegans with a y?
The way you spell could amaze John L.,
The Sullivan with an i.
Margaret Sullavan, star alone,
Spell it your own sweet way;
The fairest of sights in twinkling lights
Is Sullavan with an a.

(from an unpublished letter to Margaret Sullavan, first quoted in Haywire *by Brooke Hayward, New York: Alfred A. Knopf, 1977)*

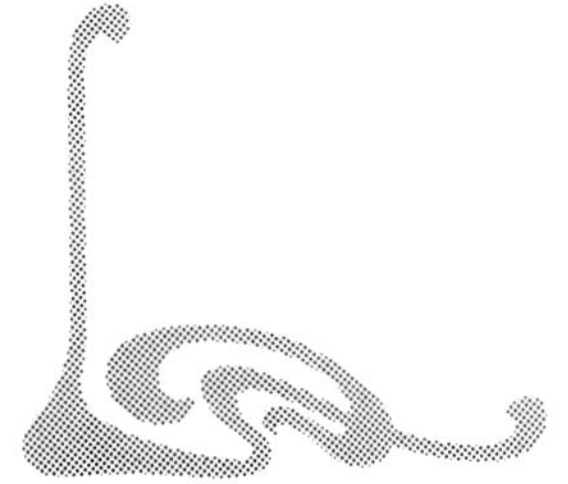

In Hollywood
by Ian Whitcomb

Where is the place that they all like to go?
It's Hollywood.
Jack and Jill, Bruce and Bill, Manny and Moe
Go Hollywood.
Down on the Boulevard Saturday night,
You've never seen such a colorful sight
But make sure that you roll up your windows real tight
In Hollywood.

Where are there so many hustling stars?
In Hollywood.
Stuck in the sidewalk or parking your cars
That's Hollywood.
Most every moment you'll hear sirens scream;
Follow the cop cars—you'll soon reach the scene
And you're bound to end up on a slab or a screen
In Hollywood.

In the tradition of countless marines—
Go Hollywood.
Tuck your equipment in super-tight jeans—
Go Hollywood.
Saunter the Boulevard, you're out for hire;
Milk all you can out of old men's desire,
'Cos in just a few years you'll find *you* are the buyer—
That's Hollywood!!

(reprinted from Lotusland *by Ian Whitcomb, London: Wildwood House, 1979)*

Mae West

Mae West: The Woman behind Diamond Lil
by Wes D. Gehring

Mae West didn't just
Enter a room,
She dusted off all the
Corners on the way through.

If she had been
Born on the frontier
It would have been
A real wild, wild West.

As it was, 30s America
Found Mae ever so steamy,
Though some merely
Called her seamy.

And at a time when censors
Tried to keep at least
One foot on the ground,
Her observations were strictly horizontal.

Mae had so much It
That Clara Bow should
Have demanded a recount . . .
Or a new nickname.

While built like a cast iron
Hour glass, Mae was male
In her mannerisms—especially
"Frank" in her suggestions.

Though seldom compared to
Depression rival Snow White,
Mae once admitted to being
As pure as the driven snow . . . until she drifted.

She had a moving impact
On "mankind," no doubt
Inspired by the image
Of Sir Thomas More—A Man for All Seasons.

Thus Mae was more than
A mere sex symbol,
In time America called
Her a real life preserver.

(reprinted from The Journal of Popular Film and Television, *Vol. X, No. 1, Spring 1982, page 72)*

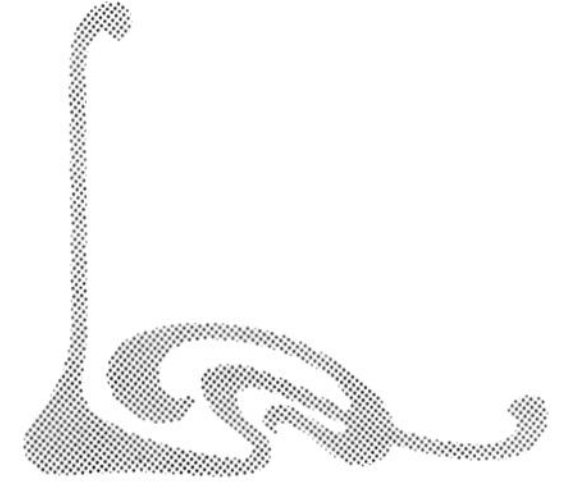

Twice as Many Gorillas
*for Ava Gardner**
by Jack Skelley

Now listen here, Guinevere, one more shot
like that you're inside the lizard noose,
I'll string you up with the iguana, or ship
you to a convent—see if you can get
the cleric's collar off your neck when you're
frazzled, spooked, and all played out.
No more midnight swims with your two handy men
and beach boy lancelots, Mister Urge and Purge.
Admit it baby, you begin your nightly
scenes with traces of a noble Spanish accent,
but soon you've dropped it altogether, sometimes
snarling a remark in Spanish slang, trotting
around the animal compound in high heels.
And by the end you're a dancing barefoot contessa,
your fingernails just exuding pearls
of take-me/forsake-me polish, as your curls and earrings
and black satin skirt make shakey orbits
around the one salacious plea your eyes
can offer. You have a plan for every
sleeping purpose: to rouse it until another
victim comes slinking back, expecting
some damage in the dark and then some rest.
Yes, I know the businessman master planner
made us all monkeys' uncles with our urges,
but you have twice as many gorillas
bounding through your supposedly civilized brain,
and you can't soothe them 'till they break the bars,
make a mess, and cower back inside again.

(reprinted from Monsters *by Jack Skelley, Los Angeles: Little Caesar Press, 1982)*

*Skelley's poem is a composition of scenes gleaned from a biography of Ava Gardner.

Motion Pictures
by Tom Wayman

Of all locations to park, my car prefers
country drive-in theatres:
those fields fenced off in the dusk
echoing with the noise of speakers attached to poles
where every vehicle faces the same way
except a few pickups
containing hardy individuals settled down in the back
under coats and blankets.
           My car especially enjoys
films about characters on the road
that include travelogue sequences as filler:
shots of strange North American cities
or European landscapes my car will never visit.
My car likes to observe these distant places
without having had to roll that far,
pistons rising and plunging,
all systems functioning, alert
for any failure.
What my car isn't happy about
are chase scenes: vehicles smashing
together, or swerving onto sidewalks
or down embankments to end in flames.
My car has passed too many overturned trucks
and police flares at other accidents
to successfully remind itself this is just a movie.
And my car seems indifferent
if the plot involves only people
indoors. But when this occurs
it loves to look higher than the screen
and the hills around,
up at the massed stars,
and recollect certain nights
it spent away out on the earth
in gear and travelling.
           My car is always a little regretful
when the films conclude
and it has to get in line
down the usual hard highway.

(reprinted from The Hudson Review, *Vol. XXXVII, No. 1, Spring 1984)*

The Death of Marilyn Monroe
by Sharon Olds

The ambulance men touched her cold
body, lifted it, heavy as iron,
onto the stretcher, tried to close the
mouth, closed the eyes, tied the
arms to the sides, moved a caught
strand of hair, as if it mattered,
saw the shape of her breasts, flattened by
gravity, under the sheet,
carried her, as if it were she,
down the steps.

These men were never the same. They went out
afterwards, as they always did,
for a drink or two, but they could not meet
each other's eyes.

           Their lives took
a turn—one had nightmares, strange
pains, impotence, depression. One did not
like his work, his wife looked
different, his kids. Even death
seemed different to him—a place where she
would be waiting
and one found himself standing at night
in the doorway to a room of sleep, listening to a
woman breathing, just an ordinary
woman
breathing.

(reprinted from The Dead and the Living *by Sharon Olds, New York: Alfred A. Knopf, 1984)*

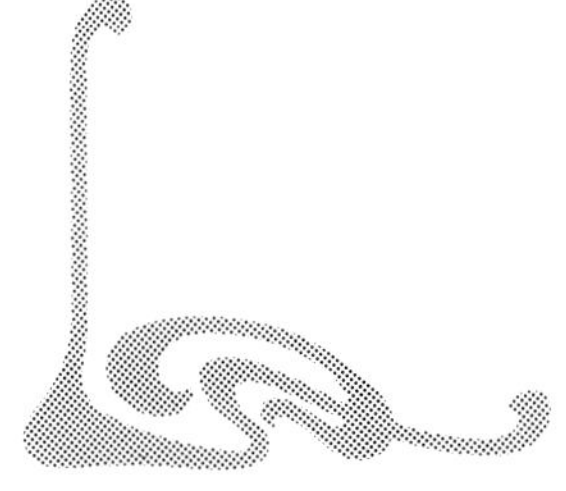

Esther Ralston

Ode to the Silents
by Esther Ralston

When I was growing up,
Those movie stars I love
Were wondrous Gods and Goddesses
Descended from above.
The "Black Pirate" really thrilled me
Swashbuckler of the Sea!
When Douglas Fairbanks bravely fought,
I dreamed he fought for me!

Theda Bara . . . Colleen Moore . . .
Herbert Rawlinson . . .
Bebe Daniels . . . Richard Dix . . .
Wasn't Harry Langdon fun?

Lillian and Dorothy . . .
Those lovely sisters Gish . . .
Betty Bronson as "Peter Pan" . . .
Fulfilling every wish.
Pearl White . . . forever perilled!
Buster Keaton's frozen pan . . .
Though Jackie Coogan haunts me . . .
I'm still Baby Peggy's fan.

Mary Pickford's golden curls . . .
And tender childlike grace,
These memories that warm my heart
No others can replace.

Lon Chaney as "The Hunchback"!
Valentino's sultry tricks!
That charming "It" Girl Clara Bow . . .
The joys of silent flicks!

Then talkies came . . . and somehow
Illusion reigned no more . . .
For even Charlie Chaplin soon
Became . . . "the boy next door!"

(specially written for this volume; Esther Ralston was a major Paramount star of the Twenties, whose films include Peter Pan *[1925],* A Kiss for Cinderella *[1925],* The American Venus *[1926],* Old Ironsides *[1926], and* The Case of Lena Smith *[1929])*

Chapliniana

One, two, three, four,
Charlie Chaplin went to war.
He taught the nurses how to dance,
And this is what he taught them:
Heel, toe, over we go.
Heel, toe, over we go;
Salute to the King
And bow to the Queen
And turn your back on the Kaiserine.

For the moon shines bright on Charlie Chaplin
His shoes are cracking
For want of blacking
And his little baggy trousers they want mendin'
Before they send him
To the Dardanelles!

Charlie Chaplin, meek and mild,
Took a sausage from a child.
When the child began to cry,
Charlie slapped him in the eye.

(These three items relating to Charlie Chaplin originated in the United Kingdom, and illustrate the comedian's appeal. The first two date from the First World War, while the last, from the twenties was sung by children to the tune of "Gentle Jesus.")

Uncle Carl Laemmle*

Uncle Carl Laemmle
Has a very large faemmle.

*This verse, which refers to nepotism within the Universal Studios of Carl Laemmle, is often attributed to Ogden Nash. However, Curtis Brown, representing the estate of Nash, reports it has no record of it.

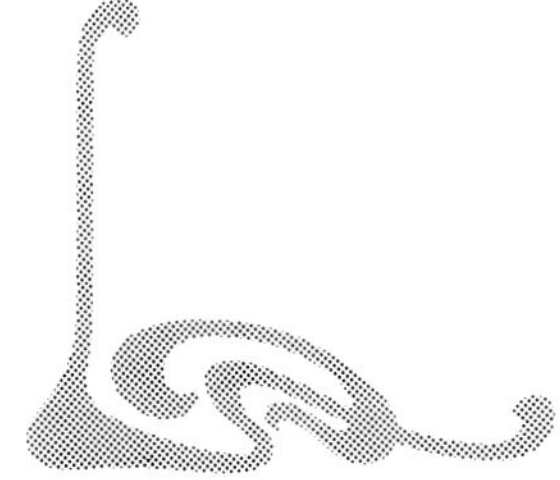

Max Ophuls
by James Mason*

I think I know the reason why
Producers tend to make him cry.
Inevitably they demand
Some stationary set-ups, and
A shot that does not call for tracks
Is agony for poor dear Max,
Who, separated from his dolly,
Is wrapped in deepest melancholy.
Once, when they took away his crane,
I thought he'd never smile again.

*James Mason was the star of two American features, *Caught* and *The Reckless Moment* (both 1947), directed by German-born Max Ophuls. The publication source of this verse is unknown.

Cecil B. DeMille

Cecil B. DeMille
Much against his will,
Was persuaded to leave Moses
Out of the Wars of the Roses.

(author and origin unknown)

The Psalm of Cinema

I am celluloid, not steel.
I am fragile yet a thing of life and beauty.
I front dangers frequently as I travel the whirling wheels of a projector.
O'er the sprockets held tight by the idlers I am forced by the motor's might.
If a careless hand mistreats me I have no alternative, I must perish.
When the pull on the take-up reel is too violent, I am torn to shreds.
If dirt collects in the aperture, my film of beauty is scratched and marred, oil soaked, my luster fades, I am no longer a beautiful picture.
I lose my desire to please people, gathering filth and grime about me.
I travel many miles in tin cans, I am tossed about heedlessly by expressmen and truck drivers.
Speed me on my way but protect me.
Bind me snuggly with my band and fasten the string securely, others are waiting to see me.
Hold me too long and I am lost forever to the waiting audience.
Have a heart for the other fellow who is waiting.
Think of my owner who will get the blame if I am late.
I am a delicate ribbon of film . . . misuse me and I disappoint thousands, cherish me and I delight and instruct the world.
I am eagerly trying to do my share in these trying times.
May I ask your cooperation in seeing that I live a life of usefulness.

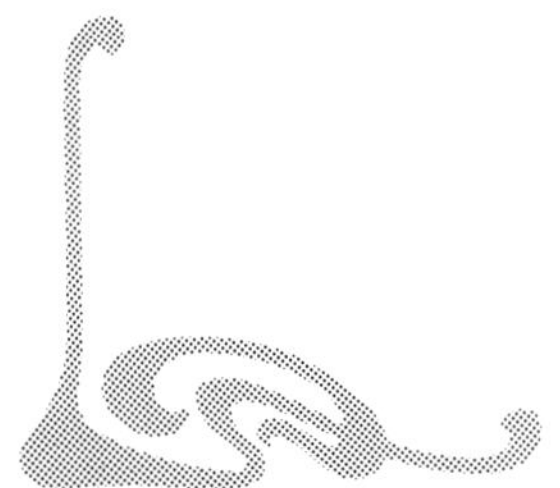

The Film Prayer

I am celluloid, not steel; O God of the machine, have mercy.
I front dangers whenever I travel the whirring wheels of the mechanism.
Over the sprocket wheels, held tight by the idlers, I am forced by the
motor's might. If a careless hand misthreads me, I have no alternative
but to go to my death. If the pull on the take-up reel is too violent,
I am torn to shreds. If dirt collects in the aperture, my film of
beauty is streaked and marred, and I must face my beholders—a thing
ashamed and bespoiled. I travel many miles in tin cans. I am tossed
on heavy trucks, sideways and upside down. See that I don't become
bruised and wounded beyond the power to heal. I am a delicate ribbon of
film—misuse me and I disappoint thousands; cherish me, and I delight
and instruct the world.

(The origins and dates of these two very similar items are unknown)

Additional Poetry on the Motion Picture

Dobyns, Stephen, "What You Have Come To Expect," in *The New Yorker*, July 14, 1980, page 36.

Duncan, Robert, "Ingmar Bergman's Seventh Seal," in *The Opening of the Field*. New York: New Directions, 1973.

Dunn, Douglas, "I Am a Cameraman," in *The New Yorker*, June 2, 1973, page 36.

Hollander, John, "To the Lady Portrayed by Margaret Dumont," in *Movie-Going and Other Poems*. New York: Atheneum, 1958.

______, "Movie-Going," in *Movie-Going and Other Poems*. New York: Atheneum, 1958.

Kumin, Maxine, "At a Private Showing in 1982," in *The New Yorker*, September 27, 1982, page 48.

Kunitz, Stanley, "The Magic Curtain," in *The New Yorker*, February 6, 1971, page 34.

Morgan, Paula, "George C. Scott," in *Say Yes!* New York: Quadrangle/The New York Times Book Co., 1977.

O'Hara, Frank, "To the Film Industry in Crisis," in *Meditations in an Emergency*. New York: Grove Press, 1957.

______, "Lana Turner Has Collapsed," in *Lunch Poems*. San Francisco: City Lights Books, 1964.

Prospere, Susan, "Moving Pictures," in *The New Yorker*, January 6, 1986, page 75.

Rigsbee, David, "Autobiography," in *The New Yorker*, August 26, 1985, page 30.

Shattuck, Roger, "The Shirt," in *The New Yorker*, October 17, 1983, page 52.

Sissman, L.E., "The West Forties: Morning, Noon, and Night," in *The New Yorker*, March 5, 1966, page 42.

Wojan, David, "The Man Who Knew too Much," in *The New Yorker*, February 8, 1982, page 42.

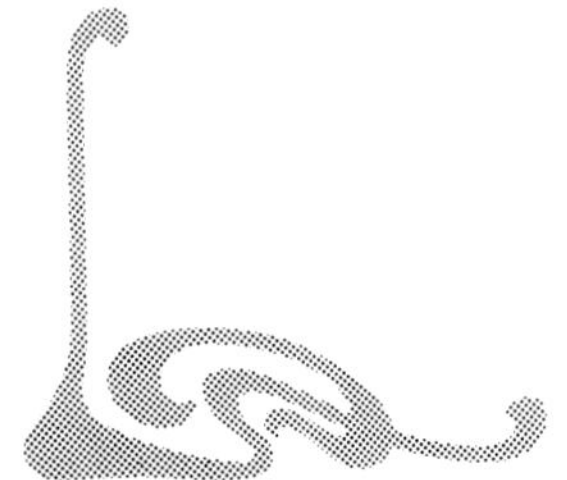

Index by Author

Subject Index

THE PICTURE DANCING ON A SCREEN:

Poetry of the Cinema

Composed by Eastern Graphics in 12 point Garamond Light,
2 points leaded, with display lines in Garamond Light.
Cover design by James Weaver Graphic
Design, Binghamton, NY

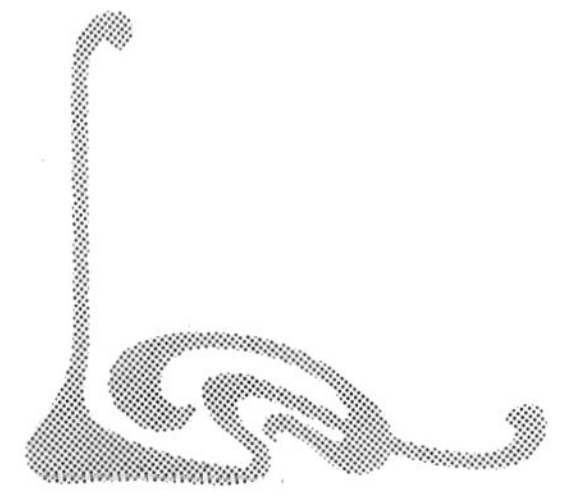